On the Essence of Language
and the Question of Art

Martin Heidegger

On the Essence of Language and the Question of Art

Edited by Thomas Regehly

Translated by Adam Knowles

polity

Originally published in German as *Zum Wesen der Sprache und Zur Frage nach der Kunst* © Vittorio Klostermann GmbH, Frankfurt am Main, 2010

This English edition © Polity Press, 2022

Polity Press
65 Bridge Street
Cambridge CB2 1UR, UK

Polity Press
111 River Street
Hoboken, NJ 07030, USA

ISBN-13: 978-1-5095-3598-9

A catalogue record for this book is available from the British Library.

Library of Congress Control Number: 2022939683

Typeset in 10.5 on 12 pt Times New Roman by
Cheshire Typesetting Ltd, Cuddington, Cheshire
Printed and bound in Great Britain by TJ Books Ltd, Padstow, Cornwall

The publisher has used its best endeavors to ensure that the URLs for external websites referred to in this book are correct and active at the time of going to press. However, the publisher has no responsibility for the websites and can make no guarantee that a site will remain live or that the content is or will remain appropriate.

Every effort has been made to trace all copyright holders, but if any have been overlooked the publisher will be pleased to include any necessary credits in any subsequent reprint or edition.

For further information on Polity, visit our website: politybooks.com

Contents

The Word. On the Essence of Language

Word – Sign – Conversation – Language

I. THE WORD AND LANGUAGE

II. THE SIGN (ITS ESSENCE BOUND TO THE EVENT)

III. THE WORD. CONVERSATION AND LANGUAGE

IV. THE WORD
(CF. POETIZING AND THINKING)

V. THE WORD AND LANGUAGE

VI. WORD AND "LANGUAGE"

VII. THE ESSENTIAL PREVAILING OF THE WORD

VIII. IMAGE AND SOUND – THE SENSIBLE

IX. LANGUAGE

X. LANGUAGE

ADDENDA

Contents

PART TWO: ON THE QUESTION OF ART

GLOSSARIES

Translator's Introduction

The present volume contains notes, sketches, and sections of fully articulated treatises, which provide unique insight into the development of Heidegger's thinking on language and art in the 1940s. The German-language reader of this text might be inclined to describe Heidegger's writing in this volume with one particularly vivid adjective: *wortkarg*. Roughly translated, *wortkarg* means sparse with words, with *karg* meaning stingy, austere, and meager. A patch of soil that is *karg* is barren, desolate, and unyielding. Heidegger's language in this text is marked by a distinct barrenness. It is a language hewn down to the bone, with all unnecessary adornments stripped away. If the language is evocative or is even pleasant to read, then it is evocative and pleasant in the same way that a barren landscape might be pleasant to look at. Gazing at a barren landscape, the viewer is taken as much by what is there as by what is *not* there. Heidegger's spare prose is not a language that seeks to reach the flowery heights of the German language, but is instead the language of the roots. A writer of different inclinations might seek to use the German language to soar. With Heidegger, one trudges and plods open a rocky landscape, coursing through a barren terrain of sparse words. The task of the translator is to render that sparseness without filling it up with too many expository accoutrements – which creates a delicate balancing act when the task of the translator is also to render comprehensible *philosophical* prose.

Heidegger's cultivation of a sparse language creates a number of distinct challenges for the translator of this phase of Heidegger's writing. While many portions of the book consist of fully formulated manuscripts, other sections contain fragmentary formulations, sentences with a loose structure, and paths of thought which Heidegger intentionally leaves incomplete. Consequently, the fragmentary nature of the original text does not so much reveal a work that is incomplete, but instead one that is intentionally left open ended. I have attempted to replicate the open-ended nature of the work, but my first priority was always to produce a readable text in English. Hence, where necessary, I have furnished fragmentary sentences with finite verbs or missing parts and have broken up long sentences, which threatened to tax the limits of English syntax.

My decisions were guided by a fundamental distinction evident in the styles of writing Heidegger employs in the present volume. In the sections formatted as paragraphs and consisting primarily of complete sentences, I generally transformed the occasional fragmentary sentences Heidegger employs into complete sentences for the sake of rendering a comprehensible philosophical analysis. In the sections which consist of lists or series of fragments, I endeavored to maintain the sparse and barren nature of the prose as much as possible and left the fragmentary in its original state. This applies especially to §§ 149–163 in the notes on language. My goal in these sections was to keep the strangeness of the original intact. This allows the reader to experience the barrenness of Heidegger's prose without sacrificing comprehensibility in the more fully fleshed-out sections of analysis.

For the sake of readable English, I was unable to maintain another peculiarity which runs throughout the text. Often, Heidegger creates sentences beginning with interrogatory words and formulated grammatically as questions, though they are not furnished with a question mark. These formulations intensify the sense of inquisitive open-endedness, which characterizes the text as a whole. For the most part, I have furnished these sentences with a question mark and rendered them as fully formed questions. Additionally, in many sections the title of the section serves as the beginning of the first sentence of the section. Given that the English sentence structure does not lend itself to replicating the order of the German sentence, it was often not possible to put the phrase from the title as the first element in the English sentence. Consequently, I was forced to abandon this feature for the most part and to start each section with a new sentence by imbedding the title in the sentence.

Individual terminological decisions are detailed in the Glossary at the conclusion of the book. The Glossary indicates the basic translation for a term; where situational flexibility demanded a different formulation, I varied from the basic translation. A few remarks are in order about fundamental terms in this work. Although they have their justified detractors, I followed two terminological decisions now common in many translations of Heidegger: (1) I translate *Anfang* and its cognate terms as "inception." (2) I translate *Ereignis* and its cognate terms with the basic translations of "event," "event of appropriation," and, in the verb form, "happening of the event." There is often no general felicitous rendering of the permutations of these terms and, while a translator might be tempted to render them with an array of different terms according to each unique setting, it is also necessary to situate this translation within the now well-established terminology used to render Heidegger in English. Employing the basic translations mentioned above risks lending a certain rigidity to the text, but it has the advantage of situating the translation within the formidable traditions of translating Heidegger.

A few remarks regarding specific terminological decisions in this text are in order. First, and perhaps most importantly, given the centrality of the word "word" in Heidegger's analysis of language, is Heidegger's play with the two plural forms of "word [*Wort*]." German possesses two plural forms of "word [*Wort*]": *Wörter* and *Worte*. *Wörter* indicates the totality of a language's lexicon. Hence, a dictionary is called a *Wörterbuch* and not a *Wortebuch*. *Worte* generally refers to a specific collection of words and would be used to render phrases such as the "words of Hamlet" or "words of a sentence." Heidegger draws a consistent distinction between the two plurals, which I have rendered by translating "*Wörter*" as "vocabulary" and "vocabulary words" and "*Worte*," the generic plural, as "words." This distinction is complicated by the further fact that the singular "*Wort*" also refers to a dictum or saying, applying to locutions such as "a word from Shakespeare," which of course refers to a phrase or plurality of words and not a single word. Heidegger's frequent use of the singular "word" ought to be read as resonating with this plurality. Throughout this text, Heidegger tends to associate "*Wörter*" (vocabulary) with the decline or downfall of language, linking it with a number of phenomena such as discourse (*Rede*), drivel (*Faselei*), the forgetting of being, the use of language as a tool, and logic. On the other hand, Heidegger associates *Worte* with terms such as saga (*Sage*), the mantra (*der Spruch*), saying (*das Sagen*), language (*die Sprache*), the authentic word (*das eigentliche Wort*), the inception (*der Anfang*), conversation (*das Gespräch*), the essential prevailing of the word (*Wesung des Wortes*), poetry (*Dichten*), and the event (*Ereignis*).

A somewhat awkward neologism was unavoidable, given that it is a precise rendering of the German original: isses [*istet*]. To create this term Heidegger plays with the third-person singular indicative form of the irregular verb "to be [*Sein*]": "is [*ist*]." He treats the third-person singular form as if it were derived from a correlating infinitive of a regular verb (to is; *isten*) and then conjugates that hypothetical

xvi   *Translator's Introduction*

infinitive in third-person singular. The outcome is the conjugated verb *istet* used to refer to the being of the beyng of beings. Heidegger uses this term both intransitively and transitively, i.e. with and without a direct object, combining it at times with "beyng" and "refusal" as direct objects. In German, copula verbs such as "to be" are strictly intransitive, meaning that they take no direct object. The use of the transitive with a form derived from a copula verb lends the construction an air of intentional uncanniness.

I follow the now well-established convention of employing "beyng" to render Heidegger's use of the antiquated spelling of "*Sein*" as "*Seyn*," while rendering the singular "*das Seiende*" as "beings," as opposed to the cumbersome yet more literal rendering of "that which is." "Dasein" has been left untranslated, except in a few instances where Heidegger divides the component parts of the word into "there [*Da*]" and "being [*sein*]." Heidegger frequently uses hyphens to draw terminological distinctions in words such as "Da-sein," always placing the hyphens in the natural breaks between parts of words (e.g. *Auseinander-setzung*; *Ver-ab-redung*). Where the English word lends itself to hyphenation between the parts of the words, I have done so, as for example in the cognate forms of in-ception (*An-fang*). Where the chosen English term does not allow for a hyphenation in the natural joints of the word (e.g. *Ver-ab-redung* as "appointment"), I have indicated Heidegger's use of the hyphen by putting the original German word in brackets.

The series of cognate terms related to the adjective *heiter* play a significant role in the text: *heiter, die Heitere, das Heitere, das Heiternde*, and *heitern*. *Heiter* as a modern adjective means merry, joyful, bright, amusing, and serene. For example, it is a common term employed in weather forecasts and promises a day of pleasant weather. I translate the adjective as "radiant." The generic neuter collective form *das Heitere* (literally: what is *heiter*, that which is *heiter*) is related to that adjective and is translated as "radiance." *Das Heitere* is not to be confused with the somewhat antiquated feminine noun *die Heitere*, which refers to a luminescence or brightness. I have thus translated *die Heitere* consistently as "resplendence." Heidegger often uses the nominalized active participle form of verbs such as *das Heiternde*, derived from the infinitive form *heitern* (meaning: to make *heiter*), which is likewise somewhat antiquated. I translate the infinitive form as "to quicken," rendering the active participle form "*das Heiternde*" as "the quickening" or "the quickening element."

I would like to thank Richard Polt and Arun Iyer for their generous assistance with unraveling tricky passages. My gratitude as well goes to the many translators of Heidegger who have come before me and paved the way across the rocky paths. I have benefited immensely from their pathbreaking efforts.

Adam Knowles
Zürich, Switzerland
March 2022

Part One

On the Essence of Language

The Saga

1. The Resolution

That *is* what needs no effectiveness in order to be.
And hence
There is a courageousness
which can even forego heroism.

Essential thinking is contained in these two sentences;
saying out of nihilation.
Nihilation as leaping in.

2. The Characteristics of the Decision

Whether one only reports from the domain of beings and plans in relation to beings.

Whether one, turned toward beings as a whole, implements such reports and plans with what "is" in all metaphysics – with "ideas" or with the "elemental," both of which are then consequently called "values."

Whether one is compelled to say beyng, even if only because he questions beyng and no longer appeals to any beings nor to beingness (to values).

To found something which is not calculated in terms of an effect and which can wait for a long time until its non-actuality itself illuminates as beyng itself, so that concealment as the event lets everything become something that is.

Beyng does not require beings, through which it might somehow "prove effective."

"Effect" is not essential to it.

But why has metaphysics posited the essence of being (beingness) into actuality and simultaneously interpreted actuality as objectivity?

Because it is never capable of thinking concealment as the event of appropriation.

3. The Question of Being

What are beings? Beings themselves are beings. Beings themselves are in being [*ist seiend*]; they are in beingness; beingness is being.

And what is being? What is it *that* beings are in this way? What is the what-being [*Was-sein*] of beings? This: *that* they are. What beings are is that they are [*Daß-sein*].

And to say that being (and not in the first place that beings are) is, "what" does that mean? (Presencing – visibility – ἰδέα – οὐσία; yet for Aristotle πρώτη οὐσία is τόδε τι.)

Questioning in this way, the question of being asks after beings at times in an unambiguous and clear manner, at times in a confused and vacillating manner, in that it asks *what* beings are.

Yet how is it decided or does it even become binding without further consideration, that being must be or even could be inquired into in terms of the what-question and what is yielded by that question?

From where does the question: *What is* … take its primacy? Is this the question of essential prevailing? Why τί ἐστιν?

Does the original inceptual thinking of Parmenides and Heraclitus and the saying of Anaximander inquire in the sense of τί ἐστιν τὸ ὄν?

They speak of ὄν and name τὰ ὄντα – but the what-question as such is not developed.

What is being asked after when the *what* is addressed?

Prior to the "what" and within the "what" as the manner of inquiry [*An*frage], that which comes to presence itself already stands in its (root-bearing) emergence standing back within itself – φύσις.

In the saying of the being of beings, φύσις already says itself, so that ἀλήθεια itself cannot be distinguished from it.

And this pro-clamation and pro-position emerging out of ἀλήθεια, which is φύσις itself, is the first saying [,][1] the *gathering* into presencing and hence the saying *of the one*, and thus the *one* is a preliminary name for beings as a whole – ἕν καὶ πᾶν – the one as unity and thus all in its allness.

---

[1] {TN : the original sentence is lacking a comma here. After consultation with Thomas Regehly, editor of the original manuscript, it was decided to render the sentence with an implied comma.}

4. The Question of Being
(The First and the Other Inception)

The question of being is recognized in its ambiguity by distinguishing the question concerning the being of beings (or concerning beingness) from the question concerning the truth of being.

Even if this other form of questioning is admitted, it still appears as nothing more than a reflected supplement to the determination of the being of beings; a supplement which only asks how "*we*" are capable of understanding (of projecting) being? Thus all that remains is nothing more than some arbitrary form of the conditional or unconditional transcendental question.

What is the decisive twist here?

In the essence of truth and of the mode of relation to it: not νοεῖν and re-presentation of that which appears, rather Da-sein in the clearing; but Da-sein at the same time as the essential prevailing of beyng and being human is otherwise, due to thrownness into Da-sein.

None of this can be achieved through "views" and "doctrines," for it can only be experienced as the history of being and in the first place in the plight of the abandonment of beings by beings.

But whether this plight compels?

Yet to what extent is the attempt to dispel the ambiguity through phrases such as "Being and Thinking" and "Being and Time" already misleading? For it insinuates that "being" is ultimately being thought in the same way here, albeit simply from a different perspective of projection. But in "Being and Thinking," being is the beingness of beings, and is experienced from out of beings; in "Being and Time," in contrast, being takes its definitive force from the truth of beyng.

"*Time*" is *not only*, as it initially seems, the prior condition of projection for thinking *as the re-presentation and making present of that which is present as such*; that is only the metaphysical-historical impetus for the transition into beyng-historical thinking, but not the essential apprehension of beyng itself.

The characterization of the distinctiveness of the question of being in terms of the differentiation between the guiding question and the fundamental question (1935ff.)[2] always has a merely propaedeutic character, and in truth it drags beyng-historical thinking back into metaphysics. But this danger looms over all transitional thinking.

---

[2] Martin Heidegger, *Introduction to Metaphysics*, trans. Gregory Fried and Richard Polt, 2nd edn. (New Haven, CT: Yale University Press, 2014), 21.

5. The Two Leaps in the Attempt to Think Being

The first leap ("Being and Time" and everything else written before 1931) is within the domain of traditional metaphysics, with metaphysics understood as the question concerning the being of beings as such as a whole. Here the task is to inquire into the meaning (the realm of projection) of being by reaching beyond the question of the being of beings, and thus to establish the foundation of metaphysics in a repetition. The inquiry into the question of being thereby understood itself to be more originary; consequently, the mode of questioning was still that of metaphysics: inquiring into the grounds of the conditions of possibility of the truth of being. Admittedly, the relation to being is already what is decisive here, and with it being itself; yet this remains and remained obscured.

The second leap is the crucial insight that the questioning involved here is already not only more originary, but also completely different, arising from another inception, and that it must now be asked in its own manner – developed from beyng itself; no longer from beings and directed toward them. Now, indeed, everything relating to the first leap remains essential; yet it is all transformed. The overcoming of metaphysics is revealed. The saying itself is distinct and is now above all merely preparatory – it is no longer philosophy (metaphysics).

Even when one knows and believes that he knows where his thinking is heading, he does not know it after all; the one single task that is to be thought is at once so concealed and yet so near: beyng.

6. The Three Insights and Knowledge

The insight awakens:
1. Being essences in the clearing of time.
2. For this something quite unique, though hitherto concealed, must also essence: Da-sein.
3. The truth of being, for which "time" is a first name, gives metaphysics not only a more originary ground.

Knowledge is bestowed:
1. Beyng brings forth the essence of [*erwest*] truth.
2. Truth attunes the "essence" through the voice of beyng.
3. Beyng is what essentially prevails and yet is not what is highest – indeed it is utterly beyond measure.

7. Beyng, "Spirit," Cognition

Truth is in beyng and as beyng in the sense of the clearing and is thus the possible essential prevailing of Da-sein, which becomes a necessity if beyng demands the grounding of its truth.

Cognition arises neither from spirit nor from the "subject," nor does "consciousness" arise from "nature."

Truth and hence the possibility of cognition are appropriated solely within beyng.

It is only for metaphysics that all of this looks different, so that even the explanation of cognition is relegated to "psychology."

Beyng, however, is nothing spiritual, nothing material, is neither "real" nor "ideal," neither conditioned nor unconditioned.

8. The Saga

The saga is the history of beyng bound to the word in the word of *thinking*. The saga names beyng, decided inceptually out of its essence, but, in contrast to metaphysics, it does not reach beyng subsequently and derivatively on the basis of some being that has already been posited, and then in turn, offer it up to beings once again as the explanatory condition of beings.

On its face, the saga encompasses "thinking" in such a way that thinking first determines itself as the steadfast naming of beyng and everywhere accomplishes this and only this, namely to remain an occasion for the essential transformation of the relation of the human to beyng, a transformation which is nonetheless the appropriative event and is never something accomplished by humans.

The saga of the history of beyng even belongs in this history because the saga bespeaks the word of being.

Saga here is not some kind of subsequent report and is not narration.

But the saga is also not the poetic word, but rather the history of beyng and specifically the pre-history of its other inception where that which is inceptual is first revealed as such.

The overcoming of metaphysics belongs at the same time to the "history of beyng": the undoing of the beingness of beings and thereby of the power of beings through beyng out of its self-withholding.

The overcoming of metaphysics
The history of beyng
The saga

We are still without the inner law of the mantra for the saga of the history of beyng. But the mantras have as their only master [*Meisterin*][3] the necessity to say the selfsame evermore inceptually each time, until at last, without even remotely trying to calculate this through comparisons, *one* word finally hits the mark, a word in which the voice of beyng becomes attunement.

What is necessary is to remain untouched by the past, i.e. by the truth of beings as metaphysics, which, in its overcoming, lets the corrupted essence play out all the more, and simultaneously it leads astray into historicism (searching for influences and things to borrow from the past).

Such untouchability is the pure guarantee of the unassailability, which, to be sure, is not enough to vouchsafe the truth of beyng, but rather the stillness of the paths into abyssal ground of being, which are never to be counted.

Admittedly, untouchability by that which is past binds us into what has been and enables the experience of harkening to what, in the history of metaphysics, belongs to the intrinsic character and inception of the history of beyng.

9. The Beyng-Historical Inception

Who decides about the essence of beyng?
Who determines the truth of this decision?
Who says what is essential and what the essence supposedly "is [*sei*]?"
Who names the essence of truth?
Why must a decision transpire here?
Is there something undecided here?
And how is such a thing able to be at all?
Within what realm are we questioning when we question in this way?
Is there such a realm, then, and how does it persist?
Where do we belong as those who question in this way?
No longer does a bridge span from there to beings,
no recourse to beings can help here.
Or has everything failed us here?
Or is failure the most concealed word?
Are we attuned by the voice of this word?
And yet we stand upon the bridge to beings.
And yet we are the bridge itself between beings and beyng.

---

[3] {TN: Master (*Meisterin*) is gendered feminine.}

Uninitiated, the more inceptual inception awaits; it first returns to itself in a grounded way in that truth – which belongs to beyng – is itself appropriated by beyng so that beyng, which is only now the event of appropriation in its fullness, is inceptual.

But, as a result, it is already decided – within what belongs more thoroughly to the essential past [*Ge-weseneren*] and within what belongs even more thoroughly to a more inceptual inception [*Anfänglicheren*] – that all beings must conjoin themselves differently out of their ground, but also what is undecided *for it* prepares itself over a long duration out of the more inceptual inception, indecipherable and always intermingled with the established end of the forgotten first inception.

It is hard to know *this* undecided element of beings within beyng as it is already essentially prevailing, since this belongs to it: an abundant self-sufficiency [*Unbedürftigkeit*] in contrast to the machination which continues to dominate everything around it.

The inception usually appears to us as what precedes and approaches the end; we take the inception for the commencement of something.

But the inception essences prior to this and essences authentically by returning back into itself, grounding itself abyssally [*ab-gründet*] and spurning [*ab-weist*] any recourse to beings, but also any recourse to being as something already decided, out of a renunciation which alone emerges from the in-clination into the appropriative event of the clearing. The inception knows no haste, its "patience" also does not arise from a calculation, it is not a form of a-waiting things as the unfettered unrest of the rest-less, rather it is the quiet of restfulness itself, which bears all the bearing-out [*Aus-trag*] of possible beings.

And yet the inception cannot be thought within the concept of the unconditioned; for it is what is most conditioned of all, for it is dependent upon and affixed only within thinking according to conditions, with what makes things possible, with processes of pro-duction.

10. The History of Beyng

The first inception: The emergence of the ungrounded presencing of the unconcealment happening as event in emergence, without the ground of concealment. That is why the inception, which returns back to itself each time, must only leave behind *presencing* and establish visibility (ἰδέα) as the sign of the essence of truth.

Philo-sophy begins in the concealment of the first inception as the thinking of the beingness of beings. Philosophy is meta-physics.

Meta-physics as the truth of beings in terms of beingness dominates the history of self-withdrawing beyng. The history of this withdrawal remains concealed in the seeming insistence of beingness and of truth as correctness (certainty and value).

This history culminates in the unfolding of beingness into unconditional and ultimately inverted subjectivity (being as the will to power and as the eternal recurrence of the same).

Thus metaphysics reaches *the culmination* of its essence and becomes ready for the *relinquishing* of the *corrupted essence*, which is to be understood as "*the worldview.*"

The *transition* of metaphysics from the essence into the corrupted essence, the tossing together of everything furnished by the essence when it is interpreted in terms of its corrupted essence, drives philosophy to its end.

But in a concealed way, beings are thereby thrown into the most extreme abandonment of beings and into the possibility of grounding the truth of being. But with this abandonment, the latter already happens as an event as the history of beyng itself and with it the *overcoming of metaphysics*.

The priority of beings (as what is actual) and beingness as what is re-presented (idea – value) disintegrates, while the scaffolding still stands, and finds itself continually filled up and filled out in new ways.

The event of this concealment reaches back into the inception and with it the inception once again becomes inceptual, but at the same time inceptual in a different way.

Beyng itself rejects all supports and crutches, all expedients and blandishments, all inducements and encouragements on the part of metaphysics.

Beyng itself demands steadfastness in the still ungrounded essence of truth – thus, however, it appropriates itself as the history of the essence of unaddressed truth and as consigned to thrownness in the grounding of its essence.

Concealment of the first inception, the unrecognizable essence of metaphysics, the inability to sense that the culmination of metaphysics has already occurred, the blindness regarding the transition of its essence into its own corrupted essence, the ignorance regarding the overcoming of metaphysics, the incapacity to be touched by the other inception – all of this indeed is now history and it is now essencing as the essential happening of being itself.

The attunement of the first inception of thoughtful thinking remains concealed from us. What makes itself known as Θαυμάζειν is the attunement at the end of the first inception, the attunement at the beginning of philo-sophy, the attunement to meta-physics (cf. Winter Semster 1937/38 and the 1939 lecture "On the Fundamental Attunement of Knowledge";[4] here things are still unclear – the initial attunement and the originary-inceptual tossed together and the one interpreted as the other).

Perhaps the originary-inceptual attunement is more closely related to the attunement which attunes the other inception, namely the mood of dread. Perhaps it is more closely related than we suspect. Perhaps it is the same and yet completely different. Perhaps it is an attunement no longer comprehensible to us, we who have been corrupted by metaphysics. And the reticence of the originary-inceptual attunement is proper to its essence.

There are no "developments" and "movements" in it, no cause–effect relations. In the event of appropriation what happens in each case is nothing but a dis-placement into Da-sein, a dis-placement through which Da-sein in each case begins to expand its concealment into the clearing, yet without necessarily recognizing this or even becoming aware of it.

Dis-placement into Dasein and under-standing (*granting* standing [*Stand*-gabe] to the stead-fastness within Dasein) are in each case *prior* to what we call human history and "world" history and only know "historically."

There is no dis-placement and under-standing without in each case reaching back into the inception, austere and isolated in itself, such that any form of explanation and derivation is doomed to fail.

The *transition* of metaphysics into the other inception, in which the history of beyng as event attunes in some way, is also dis-placement – towering forth within itself from the inception and impossible to calculate in terms of any goal.

Every form of dis-placement into Da-sein is the de-parture into an inceptual property, within which the event of appropriation finds the grounding of its truth.

---

[4] Martin Heidegger, *Basic Questions of Philosophy*, trans. Richard Rojcewicz and André Schuwer (Bloomington: Indiana University Press, 1994); "Von der Grundstimmung des Wissens," Lecture from June 9, 1939, in *Vorträge*, Part 2, vol. 80.2 of *Gesamtausgabe* (Frankfurt am Main: Vittorio Klostermann, 2016), 777–788.

11. "The History of Philosophy" and the History of Being

The "History of Philosophy" is a historiographical matter, no matter in which form this "history" becomes an object of study. There are many possibilities here that have not yet been exhausted: the history of "ideas," the history of didactic doctrines, the history of "problems," the history of "spirit," the history of culture, with "philosophy" taken as a project within the history of culture. In contrast to the history of ideas, which one takes to be abstract on the basis of an inadequate concept of the "idea," one could also set about producing a history of the "blood" or the "luminescence of the blood."[5] These options, often mixed together with one another, maintain the "interest" in a constant possibility for keeping ourselves busy, even when no one is determined or compelled by thinking anymore.

The essence of history remains uncomprehended; the objectification of beings is always decisive. The essential origin of history as the essential prevailing of beyng and history as the history of beyng can never be made known in terms of the historiographical study of philosophy; the authentic ground of this impossibility lies in the fact that, if the history of beyng is experienced, then philosophy has reached its end.

12. Beyng-Historical "Thinking"

1. *is not a manner of comprehending* something – in terms of storing it away in the universal – nor in terms of *self-representation*, explanation, or being represented ("dialectics"),
2. is not *"explanation"* – production in terms of causes and the representation of causes,
3. but is also not a form of *"contemplation"* in terms of having what is present in front of us –
4. rather it is a form of distancing that does not rely upon beings (the "no"), the distancing of the event of appropriation which does not let the event escape it (rather refusal comes to a halt and enables the mode of listening appropriate to the voice of stillness); none of this is to be thought of as a removal of "the object" – rather as the happening as event "within" it, as the "in-between" *of the abyssal grounding*; *belonging in affinity* from afar, steadfastness.

---

[5] *[Cf. Alfred Schuler, *Fragmente und Vorträge aus dem Nachlass* (Leipzig: Barth, 1940).]

13. Steadfastness and Thinking
(cf. What is Metaphysics? "Theaetetus")[6]

Steadfast thinking never expresses a rigid blind adherence to what one owns, rather, as the steadfastness of Da-sein, it does not take a stand with regard to beings. It is renunciation which allows for the requisite distancing, in which the distant as distant does not escape in its approach from afar.

Steadfast thinking does not *comprehend* by covering over beyng with assertions, which inevitably accommodate what is to be thought under the cover of what has already been comprehended and what is therefore seemingly clear.

Beyng-historical thinking knows no "concepts"; the saga that is proper to it says that beyng is (saying of beyng without image and interpretation; not letting the event escape out of distancing). For this can only appear as empty uniformity to any attempt at comprehension; since the selfsame has "already been taken care of" as far as understanding is concerned

14. The "Concept" – Distancing – Naysaying

Distancing alone corresponds to the event of appropriation as abyssal grounding. This means: in the saying of beyng, it must not only be kept in active silence, but in this active silence it must first be kept in the distance of the arrival. There is no question of dragging something closer, but it is also not the morose immersion into the ir-rational, rather it is a matter of the cold audacity of knowledge of the simple, whose strict conjuncture would require a master to say:
Beyng is and *isses* [istet] *beyng.*

Beyng-historical thinking is not a form of comprehending that wrangles things together and situates them into "universals," each as a representation and product; rather it is distancing, *negating* saying.

---

[6] Martin Heidegger, "Was ist Metaphysik?" in *Wegmarken*, vol. 9 of GA (Frankfurt am Main: Vittorio Klostermann, 1976), 103–122; translated by David Farrell Krell as "What is Metaphysics?" in *Pathmarks*, ed. William McNeill (Cambridge: Cambridge University Press, 1998), 82–96; Martin Heidegger, *Vom Wesen der Wahrheit: Zu Platons Höhlengleichnis und Theätet*, vol. 34 of GA (Frankfurt am Main: Vittorio Klostermann, 1988); translated by Ted Sadler as *The Essence of Truth: On Plato's Cave Allegory and Theaetetus* (New York: Continuum, 2002).

Naysaying. By contrast, "negative theology" is *metaphysical* – a crossing out that is directed toward the ὄντως ὄν.

15. The No of Beyng-Historical Thinking

The no of beyng-historical thinking is the no which appropriates as event and belongs to beyng. It does not get involved with the insistence upon beings, nor with the dominant interpretation of beings, which is now hardly knowable; but, at the same time, it does not permit itself to lose track of that which refuses itself and holds fast in its self-refusal.

The no of beyng is attuned through the attunement of the voice of the silence of the stillness of the gentleness of the opening of appropriation.

This no is the echo of the nothing within beyng. This no can never simply be denigrated into mere negation and it does not require the initial incorporation into an affirmation.

Admittedly, the uttered "no" insinuates the thought of resistance, opposition, and rigidity all too easily; while it is more so the "opposite" that is said and, were it permitted here to explain in a rather playful manner, the no would be a "yes"; it is no "yes," rather the no as steadfastness within refusal.

If the no is the echo of the nothing within beyng and thus the echo of the nothing within the essential prevailing of beyng, then affirmative attunement to the voice and to the attunement of beyng essences within it (it is not the yes of the affirmation of beings – the actual – not saying yes to "life").

This affirmative attunement reveals itself to be the essential depth of Da-sein and reveals the ground of the historical being of the human. Here the human is situated within his own property and is thus authentic. Thus he no longer requires the self in terms of "the egological," nor in terms of the "subject," which possesses itself as "spirit" and "reason."

Affirmative attunement is essential negation – but attuning affirmation is not first a form of affirmation in which the attunement which happens as event for Da-sein is extinguished and diminished in favor of beings.

16. Naysaying and Questioning

To what extent is questioning the most prevalent attribute of thoughtful thinking? Questioning executes the disengagement from beings and contemplates beyng. Yet a particular misinterpretation constantly impedes the emphasis on questioning, namely the notion that the only thing that matters anywhere is doubt or even evasion in the face of any fixed attitude or position.

Yet that is how one measures the inquiry of beyng, in terms of the decisiveness of the procedure, which is unavoidable for the operation of beings.

If contemplated from the perspective of beyng, however, questioning is just the preliminary stage, but at the same time it is also the initial proclamation of naysaying. It is only from this point that it can first be made clear to what extent questioning is simultaneously also an answer within thoughtful thinking, i.e. the affirmative attunement to the attunement of beyng in saying.

17. The Word

The word has its essence in naming, and this is the experience of beyng. Naming is understood firstly as the appropriative event directed to the silence of the stillness of beyng. As that which is silent, naming alone can first break silence in sound. Thus the word becomes the resounding word and words arise, which, however, are gathered and unified beforehand in the essence of the word.

The human speaks without sensing that he is breaking essential silence, a silence which he is incapable of knowing. Saying arises from a rupture. And only a saying of beyng grounds a truth for beings.

The saying of beyng cannot be captured in terms of rules and cannot be activated based on models. Since it is form-less, it is obligated to forego the "methods" of "philosophy" and to leave the "systematic approach" to philosophy behind; but it is not as if these were just the external shells meant to contain arbitrary contents of thinking. To the extent that they have remained genuine, "system" and "method" have emerged solely from one singular interpretation of being (the "mathematical" interpretation, which comprehends being as "subjectivity" from the perspective of the ἰδέα). If it relies on cultivated language and practices a fastidiousness of the word, then saying has not yet found itself in its inception; for here the beauty of speech can all too easily distract from the originary dimension (i.e. its absence).

Beyng-historical thinking becomes the foreword [*Vorwort*] only initially and, with great effort, it can be permitted to offer a preliminary saying to the authentic word. Yet an initial approach of the transformation of listening directed to the saying of the thinker will be successful.

But perhaps the essence of the word must be taken in its full solemnity and a calling must be assigned to the saying, in the face of which saying cowers back in terror without even knowing that terror is perhaps the attuning element within beyng. Perhaps the word must speak back into silence, publicly inaudible and unheard-of, and thus disentangle itself from the idea that public platitudes are the measure of the truth of the word.

Perhaps the full solemnity of the active silence of beyng and of its reticence must be taken on and perhaps this mood of reticence attunes all steadfastness of being of "the" there [*Da*] – as the clearing of beyng.

Perhaps thinking stands here before the simplest step leading into a terrain whose worldliness is still entirely concealed from us.

The un-heard aspect of the word of beyng, namely that no listening could ever measure up to the task of securing and assigning the word carried along in perception [*Vernommenheit*], will also never be disturbed by being overheard. The word of beyng *is* also unheard and overheard and this word belongs to the essential prevailing of beyng itself, no matter whether, nor if it allies itself with the attuning voice. The history of beyng remains not only outside of calculation, but also outside of any intimation. At the most, this intimation is capable of thinking ahead of certain moments of the decision of the truth of beyng, but it is never capable of determining the now beforehand.

The brittleness of *thinking* is more suitable to the attunement of the voice of beyng than is any submissiveness derived from other sources.

18. Beyng and Word

Yet, if beyng is an inception and everything inceptual belongs to it, and if the inception is in each case grounded abyssally to its originlessness from the standpoint of beings, and if in such an opening of appropriation the emerging forth of beings which have hitherto been unbound creates no causality, and if the beyng of effect absconds, and if the abyssal grounding conceals itself and concealment returns reticence back to beyng, then how is any name supposed to say beyng? Every name has already broken with reticence, including "beyng." Or so it seems. And yet the knowledge of the inception still conceals this: the fact that the word essences from reticence and essential saying remains steadfast within the stillness of beyng: that beyng isses [*istet*] beyng.

Thus the word "of" beyng deprives itself of sound and of the mis-recognition of reticence.

The word "of" beyng does not insist upon resonating in the public sphere and it maintains its essence in this way: not by first being a sign and an indication, rather by being beyng itself.

19. Beyng as the Appropriating Event (The Human)

is the appropriating event of the in-between which appropriates itself.

The in-between is prior to all where and when and what and how; it can never be asked how it can be accomplished in terms of "beings"; for it "is" already accomplished, though in this case it has seemingly been abandoned.

The appropriating event is not subjectivity (as will or something of that sort), is not objectivity, is also not presencing into the unconcealed (φύσις).

It is never the case that beyng is first contemplated from the per-spective of the human; rather the human is displaced into Da-sein in advance and is appropriated over to the in-between.

Beyng is un-conditioned; but even this appellation only thinks meta-physically; in the leaping off from beings.

20. Beyng and Attunement

Beings are not things that have an effect, they are not effective and are not what is actual; beings are only that which essences in beyng. As attunement, beyng sets the pitch; beyng does not cast its pall "around" things. It only seems to do so because we misinterpret the origin of attunement. Attunement "surrounds" beings because it permeates beings and shines through beings. Determining the pitch of attunement is not a kind of effect and not at all a kind of causation. Setting the pitch is effectless, for it has no need for an effect.

Attunement possesses the essence of the opening of appropriation into what is proper; this is appropriation into the property of poverty, while poverty alone is rich enough to bestow the non-actual, i.e. to bestow what has been poetized and what is thought and thinkable in creative thinking [*Er-denken*].

But, for the most part, the human counts upon what beings "other-wise" are, i.e. in terms of what is customary for the forgetting of being, which, even though it has been consigned to being, keeps trying to calculate being anew in terms of beings.

> Beyng is what is most in being [*Seiendste*];
> but what is most in being is not a being,
> rather beyng as appropriating event.
> Beyng is beyng.

The critical engagement [*Aus-einander-setzung*] with all metaphysics is grounded in such a saga; for the saga expressly posits being in the universality of representation as such and in the supreme element of the first cause, even though it does not sufficiently ground this notion of "expressly"; within the development of contemporary metaphysics, the form of causation pertaining to all beings and thus the form of causation *pertaining to the human* as a rational creature (which thinks in concepts and likewise thinks in terms of representations of beingness) is replaced by the *construction* of the absolute and the construction within the absolute; this remains the unposed and unresolved question of anthropomorphics.

"Beyng is beyng," however, this is also distinct from the ἔστιν γὰρ εἶναι of Parmenides.

21. Beyng

Beyng is insofar as it never permits itself to be derived from beings, nor to be conditioned by things.

Insofar as it is not derived from beings and is not conditioned [*bedingt*] by things, beyng is what is not relative and in such a way it is the ab-solute [*Ab-solute*].

Insofar as it alone "authentically" "is" (isses [*istet*]), insofar as it essences as being, beyng is what is in most in being [*das Seiendste*] and is therefore precisely never a being.

In spite of this, beyng is not "God."

In spite of this, beyng cannot be let go of under the pretense of it being "what is most general [*Generellste*]."

In spite of this, it never helps to offer an explanation of being, through the elucidation of the manner in which a *human* – regarded as *animal rationale* – represents and "abstracts" being.

Yet, indeed, it is only through knowledge of the human as *animal rationale* that the question of the reference of beyng to the human and the question of the differentiation of being and beings acquires its inceptual dignity and its genuine dignity.

*

What is to be made of the seeming "neutrality" of beyng – indifferent to all beings? pure "element?"– *as if the nothing did not essence in beyng!*

The neutral *could* – but must not – ever be anything more than beings and a being.

22. The Nothing and Beyng

If only the pure nihilating nothing "were," then beyng would be obligated to reign in its sole full essential prevailing and would tear itself away into its essential prevailing. And then a being would never be capable of offering refuge to beyng and it would be possible that it (beyng) would only seemingly remain abandoned to beings. This, however, the sole essential prevailing of pure nothingness, would be the most difficult thing. Only he who thinks ahead into beyng in the wake of the overcoming of metaphysics is capable of thinking this and he who does not represent being in terms of beings (primal cause) or as directed toward beings (as their most universal attribute). Admittedly, for metaphysics it seems, and indeed it must seem, that this fact, namely the fact that nothing is, is the easiest thing and is "more likely" to be possible than the fact that beings are. For, in addition to this, the fact that beings are, they require in each case a ground and that means that they require a cause. For in addition to the fact that *beings* are, and specifically that they are unconditioned in their ground as beings, that is the first and clearest and the most necessary and hence the least questionable thing for metaphysics.

Hence Leibniz says in this context, a context which leads him to the great principle of all metaphysics (the principle of reason): *Car le rien est plus simple et plus facile que quelque chose*[7] (*Principes de la Nature et de la Grace, fondés en raison*, no. 7, vol. VI Gerhardt, p. 602; cf. "What is Metaphysics?" Conclusion).[8]

---

[7] "For nothing is simpler and easier than something." Gottfried Wilhelm Leibniz, "Principles of Nature and Grace," in *The Monadology and Other Philosophical Writings*, trans. Robert Latta (Oxford: Clarendon Press, 1898), 405–425, 415.

[8] Heidegger, "What is Metaphysics?", 96.

23. Beyng as Nothing

Beyng as nothing appropriates and appropriates the clearing;
in appropriating the clearing, it isses [*istet*] the refusal;
beyng "is" and yet is never a being;
beyng "is" because it isses [*istet*] beyng;
but beings "are" not by turning toward beyng, even if beings only appear in the clearing (within beyng) and only become present and absent in the clearing.

Beings cause the enforcement and effect, and beings are causation.

Beyng appropriates [*er-eignet*] naysaying.

24. The Nothing

Why is the nothing more originary and more essential (that which appropriates beyng more thoroughly) than "something?"

That is because the very act of comparing the two, if properly comprehended, has already decided in favor of the nothing, to the extent that nothing here says: not at all a being, rather: being.

Something is always a being, even the "*ens*" *rationis*.
But the nothing is never an *ens rationis* because it is never an *ens*.

Thus the nothing is already the word of being. But even when it is at this point, thinking merely stands at the most provisional beginning of the creative thinking of the essence of the nothing.

The nothing does not emerge through the abdication to beings, rather it is the inceptual saying of beyng, it is saying of the *naysaying* within the opening of appropriation.

25. The Event of Appropriation

By leaving itself behind deposited into its own property (the inception), the event of appropriation appropriates itself over to its essence and opens up the essential prevailing of the clearing which is bound to the in-between. This clearing only countenances con-cealment, which itself can never be established as something present.

Beyng isses [istet] *beyng* and "is" never God and beyng is never the human being and is never beings as a whole.

Beyng isses [*istet*], it preserves itself in surrendering to its essential prevailing.

The human being's lack of tranquility is never able to unsettle beyng, though this lack of tranquility can unsettle the structure of the clearing, the clearing in which beings have been compelled and solidified in the formation of their presence. The lack of tranquility is the most protracted delay which history is yet to encounter, for this lack of tranquility is the excretion of the machination into reality, with the result that beings count for what is actual.

26. Event of Appropriation

The thinking of "the" event is appropriated from the event and stands within its clearing, permeated with light and posited in a "space," which is darkness in its inceptual essence.

The thinking of the event of appropriation is not oriented toward the "ground," nor toward the conditions of possibility, freedom, representation, or selfhood. Rather, the *opening of appropriation appropriates over the ex-propriation* of all beings who might attempt to bring themselves into the form of beingness and to place their deformed figures immediately into the placeless position of beyng.

Saying assumes the appearance of "dialectics" and antitheses; listening to it in this way means clinging to the external aspect instead of listening out of the essential prevailing and standing within it.

There is also *no* "theo-sophy" here; for it is not as if beyng were now just "more a priori" (like the divinity beyond God) than beings, rather it is the "in-between"; for the event of appropriation determines another history.

27. Beyng

Beyng is the event of appropriation directed toward the property of its essential prevailing.

In this way (it) appropriates the truth.

The event of appropriation is the act of tossing asunder pure coming, of tossing asunder the essential past as it has been decided and of tossing asunder constant presencing.

Tossing asunder appropriates in the event of appropriation and "oneness" is not something above it, as if the event of appropriation could still be represented in the form of "a" being.

Oneness does not at all have priority, rather the unique singularity arises from the *collected property* [Eigen-tum] of the event of appropriation. Beyng, however, comes to be as the in-between. The in-between is the abyssal ground. It is what is indeed free of beings and free for the essential prevailing, it is unencumbered by any ground and takes a decisive stance toward grounding. Nevertheless freedom – which is also not to be understood as the capacity for the good and great – (i.e. for things that already are) – is not the inceptual essence of beyng. The event of appropriation is more inceptual than freedom.

The idea of freedom comes into being out of the metaphysics of subjectivity; similarly, the essence of the "ground" comes into being from the metaphysics of the cause (the state of being produced – ποίησις, φύσις).

*

Beyng – abyssal grounding.
Refusal of the "ground" within beings.
Settling toward the ground [*An-gründig*] as the essential prevailing of the essence of unconcealment; only then is it the renunciation of any possibility of taking refuge in ψυχή – though first a priori – pure *beyng within being* (cf. basic words "Apriori").

Beyng grounds abyssally into that which constantly directs it to the inception. Beyng grounds abyssally the decisive divide into the occasion which arises from itself.

28. Beyng, God, the Human

How does the human belong to the essential prevailing of beyng?

This question is not asked in the customary manner: what relationship does the human maintain to beings? That inceptual question thinks in a movement toward *Da-sein* and is more inceptual than reflection upon the question of whether the human still does or does not have any gods. Perhaps this quest for gods is nothing but a *belated arrival* of metaphysics.

Perhaps there are no more gods in the abyssal ground of a godlessness, a godlessness which belongs to beyng more essentially than any idolatry [*Göttertum*] does. Perhaps the twilights of the idols are nothing more than escape routes leading out of the day of "metaphysics."

If, however, there is a simple steadfast being of the human, a being which bears out beyond "divinity" and still upholds the illusion that godlessness is a lack and a mere termination of the previously great and sole possession?

29. Beyng

The historical human, who as a historical being alone lays claim to the relation to being as the essential ground, and who does so for the most part unwittingly, never experiences being, for being is not compulsion, nor power and, when it is power, then only because it has been let loose into it as a manifestation of "life," which the human himself believes himself to be and yet will never know as a form of alienation.

The gentleness and stillness of beyng, its purity as that which is inceptually "nothing," easily leads the human astray into beings and placates him with an illusion.

The reign of the illusion arises out of ungrounded beyng, for it only reveals itself as appearance and rejects its essential ground in that appearance.

Beyng "*is*" prior to the gods and prior to the human and is more inceptual than decisions about them.

30. Beyng is and only Beyng Is

Beyng is not a piece of being and not a seed of being "within" being.

Beyng is also not the objectivity impressed upon beings by representation.

Beyng is hardly presencing, in whose visibility the ready-to-hand reveals itself. Self-showing contains the first, though no longer revocable, solidification of "being" resting upon the basis of a later form of objectivity.

Beyng is inceptually the unconcealment of the upsurge (φύσις), in whose constancy (ἕν) gathering (λόγος) grounds itself, even while surging forth and back. In this gathering, the unconcealed togetherness essences and there it contains both presence and absence.

Beyng is more inceptually and adventitiously the event of appropriation. The event of appropriation grounds the proper and peculiar element (something which can essence within the property) and yet, in this grounding, beyng withdraws into the abyss and bestows the refusal.

The unique attribute of this carries belonging into the clearing of the event of appropriation. What is transferred over into the clearing discloses itself as a "being" and appears to "be" this alone, and it does so without needing beyng, which is nowhere to be found.

Beyng is and, in coming, it is the more inceptual inception.

Beyng is nothing.

Beyng in no way has nothing as its determination, and it cannot be classified in accordance with the nothing.

Beyng essences as nothing, and the nothing rejects, in a nihilatory gesture, the possibility that any "being" could become the "cause" of beyng and it rejects the possibility that representation could become the measure of beyng.

In the coming of the event of appropriation, the essential past arrives, and the essential past is the inceptual refusal of coming.

Coming and having been "are" never in a state of becoming; rather the event alone attunes the "is."

31. Abyssal Ground

Abyssal ground and abyssal grounding have their own most somber "meaning" here in beyng-historical saying, which calls for thinking the event of appropriation as the ground of Da-sein and thinking Da-sein, in turn, as the *grounding* of the clearing.

The abyssal ground, however, is this: the way in which the event of appropriation refuses *itself* in the opening of appropriation and lifts *itself* away into its own property, which is something we nonetheless only seldom know in each case in the event of appropriation.

Common opinions therefore never latch on to the word "abyss," for the abyssal calls for "profundity" and a "tragedy" plays out within it while reckoning with an "emotional impact."

None of these attributes have any influence on the tuning of the voice of beyng, which keeps silent abyssally and, in silence, it is the inception of the word.

Nor is there any "mysticism" at work here; for thinking beyng is prior to all theology and philo-sophy and hence is prior to all metaphysics.

*

The quiet tenderness of intense anguish within the event of appropriation.

To think all essential voices back into the event of appropriation.

"Anguish" – bound to the event.

Event of appropriation – it is fundamentally different from the dialectic of the unconditioned subjectivity of "reason."

32. Beyng

The purest proximity to beyng requires no intensification, for it is simply proximity and is fully distinct from any deliverance over to beings, or deliverance to the state of being "full" of being in the much-vaunted lived experience.

The proximity to being is not the act of touching beings (which one takes to be "being" by passing off the indeterminate universality of beings as being).

The proximity to being is nothing tangible at all and is not the experience of being touched.

The proximity to being is the constancy in the abysmally grounded re-fusal as the pure coming of the carrying out of the essence of what we otherwise used to deem to be the gods and of what we used to know as the human.

33. The More Inceptual Saga

That beyng (not beings) *is;*
that beyng, however, is not only presence rising up, but is also the opening of appropriation grounding abyssally;
that *the opening of appropriation* "is" and is the nothing *as* the event of appropriation.
That such a thing cannot be noticed or recorded, neither through everyday occurrences, nor through destinal sendings;
that the "is" also first determines itself out of beyng and all saying defines itself from this attunement. That such saying is prior to any "grammar."
That beyng is –
and neither beings nor non-beings can "be" without the grounding of the truth of a more inceptual beyng.
That It [Es] *appropriates itself*
(the ground of the truth of its essence), in order to ground the abyss based on this ground and to appropriate purely – and to contain every "is" within it.
That beyng is –
not only the "is" is determined by beyng, but so too is the "that," and that means to say: the not of nothing and both the not and nothing in themselves.
That beyng is – the truth of this inceptual saga bequeaths itself to the essence of beyng.

Beyng stands in distinct contrast to the originary primordial word of Parmenides: ἔστιν γὰρ εἶναι – after which immediately follows – and indeed they must follow it – the words μὴ δ᾽ εἶν᾽οὐκ ἔστιν (Peter von der Mühll).[9]

34. The Untenability of the Differentiation between "Being" and "Becoming"

There is nothing that only "becomes," rather everything "is" – not only as path and way to "being," rather as a way that is.

Everything "is" because it isses [*istet*] in beyng as event of appropriation.

"Becoming" (Hegel – Nietzsche) is only intended to unconditionally secure the state of constancy, and also to sustain the inconstant as "being," thereby elevating "becoming" to "being"; the distinction between "being" and "actuality" lends itself to this.

"Becoming," however, is determined by "negativity." Through this negativity its being-historical origin arising out of beyng comes to light all the more.

The first inception (Anaximander, Heraclitus, Parmenides) is not capable of overcoming the distinction between being and becoming, granted that it was at all thought and was not at all "indebted" to a later interpretation which was imposed upon it.

35. Truth and System

The domain of truth (as the essential prevailing of the true in terms of grounded revelation in beings) is beyng, which essences in the event of appropriation and falls short of taking on a structure. Saga is never structured. Beyng knows no σύστασις and beingness is never required to align with a system. Beyng erects itself as unconditioned subjectivity in the abandonment of beings and enables its abandonment of being to become the ground of the occurrence of history.

[9] Hermann Diels, *Die Fragmente der Vorsokratiker*, vol. 1, ed. Walter Kranz (Hildesheim: Weidmannsche Verlagsbuchhandlung, 1951), 232 (Remark to 28 B 6).

36. The Attunement of the Voice Determines

Determining attunement – does not "effect" or cause anything; does not approach beings, rather is "only" the essential prevailing of beyng itself.

Stead-fastness in attunement.

Where does the psychological-anthropological "semblance" of attunement as "feeling" and "passion," *affectus* – πάθος – come from? Because the human is only thought as *animal rationale*; from that perspective, it is all too easy to consider the human to be something *irrational*.

Anthropologism.

37. Where is a Measure?

Measure is not outside of the human being and is not inside him, but indeed it is contained in the way in which he is appropriated by beyng, to which he belongs.

In the midst of this we think we know what "outside" and "inside" mean; as if the human were a spatial and space-filling entity whose spatial limits reach their end at some point (some say on the surface of the body).

We are also inclined to say that a person is "beside himself" and this ecstatic state can indicate the reference to beyng; this kind of belief then insinuates that the human, being with himself, is as it were cut off from the human and cut off from the reference to beyng.

Yet if "ek-stasis" here means the reference to beyng, then the human first becomes human in the process of this standing out and abiding, and this in turn gives rise to the domain within which only the human is both with *himself* and can be himself.

Selfhood is of such a deep essence that the reference to I-hood [*Ichheit*] only displays a byproduct serving from time to time as a characteristic, though not as a characteristic of being a self, rather a characteristic of a special form of self-representation.

Hence it could be said, with regard to the reference to beyng, that the measure is not only outside of the human being, but that it is also within him, within beyng, to the extent that inside refers to the particular reference to beyng, which is bound to selfhood.

And yet the measure is neither for itself in the reference, nor is it in itself in beyng, if "in itself" in turn means: isolation into the discrete mode of a thing. Beyng "itself" "is" in each case as the event of appropriation and is never "in itself," not because it could ever be compared to objectivity for an act representation, but rather because beyng returns back to itself (concealment) by appropriating the human being into Da-sein (the there [*Da*] to *be* [sein]). To the extent that the human is grounded in *Da*-sein, he enters into the property of the event of appropriation, i.e. he enters into beyng itself. And, therefore, only the ground of the *human* being can be granted the name of a being in the sense in which the human *is* Da-sein (steadfast in the there). The fact that plants and animals, mountains and streams also "are," and the fact that they belong to beings in terms of this being is something quite distinct and something which cannot be elucidated based on a reversed scale of being: stone, plant, animal, human, angel, god (for here the guiding logic is "spirit" and the possession of spirit and lack of representation, or incremental stages – monadology).

But why do we seek a measure? To what extent is there the sort of thing which requires measurement?

Measure means the how much, how far, and whither of belonging; but it also means moderation, the act of taking pause within what is allotted to you, that to which the human is bequeathed as something essentially prevailing.

Taking pause is, as the steadfastness within the there [*Da*-], the preparation and preservation of the clearing of beyng, through which everything can only be entrusted to its essence from out of the word.

Such a measure as taking pause within what is allocated is only worthy of questioning if and wherever beyng itself bears the essence of a being in the act of clearing. This, however, is what is designated for the human.

Where there is a measure, there is also the proximity of *calm*, and calm is that inceptual gathering of all history within the event of appropriation.

Wherever a measure can be, only there can the measureless also be, and the measureless reaches its most extreme point in the motility of power and achieves its essence as machination.

We are still barely up to the task of thinking being, for we only know it in the mask which metaphysics has thrust upon it in the "form" of beingness, which immediately drifts away from us into withdrawal and emptiness.

Even though we have not experienced disconcertment in the face of beyng, we are still attempting to replace that empty beingness with "allegories," which thereby confirms them in the very form of essential validity which was already conceded to them; for how else could this rambling obsession with groundless and imagined allegories still unleash such busybody activity and still manage to upset the human who is unaware of how he has been cast off by being, leaving him to hunt for a "myth?"

Even if we were to concede that we no longer have a "myth," and even though this concession might be a step toward reflection, we nonetheless retract this step, even though it has hardly been attempted and we have only ventured into it blindly by remaining fixated on finding a "myth" once again, or on replacing the yet undiscovered myth with some sort of contrivance.

"Myth" has long been merely the contrary to "logos," and one understands logos in the modern era as "reason." Standing in contrast to reason, "myth" is then justifiably reduced to the "irrational." "Myth" is a word which intends to name a realm *prior* to the inceptual, a terrain where being has not yet entered the open realm. Myth always remains a "negative" term and it specifically remains in a "negativity," which always has the premise of "*ratio*" as its precondition. And thus all discussion of "myth" is simply a bad form of "rationalism," which has come off the rails. This is a rationalism which can never find a ground to support a successful decision for truth and, consequently, a decision for the essence of truth.

The pseudo-dispute about mythos and logos merely corresponds to the characteristic decisionlessness of an age in which the abandonment of beyng, though completely concealed, reaches its culmination.

38. Not What "is Coming"

Thinking involves not predicting what "is coming" in terms of the given circumstances and in terms of notable situations, rather it involves saying what occurs. This occurrence only arises from the knowledge of history; but that is beyng itself.

The initial sounding of beyng – the culmination of the truth of being as such as a whole.

The word of beyng and the experience of refusal.

39. What Are "We" To Do

What are "we" to do "in the face of" beings as the will to power?
The question is too hasty, for we are not yet in the truth, for there is only truth when occurrence is experienced as the history of beyng – let us experience what *is*!

That beyng is – and how? As beyng!

That is the "meaning" of the reflection upon "metaphysics" – meaning?!

40. Not a "New" Philosophy

The task is not teaching a "new" philosophy; not offering up a "world-view" with which one could "initiate" something practical.

What then? The slight and sole element: preparing an experience of beyng within the machination of beings. Measured by the common standards of weight, that is insubstantial enough – and yet: an inception of history emerges and that inception is only from the essential prevailing of the truth of beyng.

41. Where Do We Stand? Directed Toward the History of Beyng

We stand in the beginning of the culmination of modernity.
Which is the time-space for the determination of this "where?"
The history of the truth of beyng.
From where does this history arise?
Out of the essence and as the essential prevailing of beyng itself.
Who are we, we who are historical in this way?
Those who are destined to be the founders and guardians of this history.
From which attunement?
From the fundamental attunement of belonging to the de-cisionlessness of proximity and of the distance of God – and his essence.
Dread [*Ent-setzen*].

42. A Curious Delusion of this Age

One believes that, after using power to fortify the empire [*Reich*] from the outside, the "inner empire" could then be built up, and indeed that it must then be built up.

As if power were merely something external and as if power were not the innermost terrain of all interiority, which is then portioned out to the next cycle of modernity beforehand.

As if something "internal" could only be "placed inside," much like hanging up a gown in the closet.

The foolhardy – those who learn reflection no more from their failures then from their victories.

But all of this still belongs to the machination, which also does not shy away from donning intellectual masks and is even willing to make use of internality or even "intimacy" in order to reach the peak of its power.

Hence everything must be as it is. And one permits everyone to hustle about, to have an impact, and to feel "satisfied" with themselves.

43. Steadfastness and Duty

"Duty" is binding oneself to what is necessary, binding oneself to the law of mores which binds everyone together (in obligation) and makes them into a human.

Yet, whenever this bond is denied and everything is consigned to a blind urge for power, then what could the source of duty be? The "worldview" now only furnishes itself with the illusory essence of metaphysics (as the "validity" of the supersensible) and is only capable of enlisting know-nothings and those who aspire to know nothing, as they are called.

There is never any duty "in itself." Duty "in itself" is simply a nullity, and wherever it is discussed, only the manner of speaking counts for anything anymore and the attempt to secure something from the past, which, in a hollowed-out state, goes on trying to salvage its mere operation for the next project and posits claims to power in a form of pseudo-validity.

Where there is no longer any belief, where there is only belief in faith, and where the empty togetherness of everyone counts for more than the "individual," there the talk of "duty" is counterfeit.

There is only duty where there is the highest freedom, which comes from granting oneself the law; otherwise, "duty" is only the name of the "moral" accoutrements of compulsion in which even morality has been denied in advance. Only the jumbled confusion of thoughtless people, people who are no longer capable of knowing anything about the pre-decided ground-lessness of the modern human being, can still try – behind all the talk of "duty" – to talk themselves into an attempt to justify a form of action whose meaninglessness only remains concealed because there is no longer any question of meaning and because the decisive conviction necessary for grounding any meaning is completely lacking.

This, however, is more obligatory than any form of duty: remaining steadfast within the question-worthiness of being and experiencing how only the cold audacity of thinking and the incorruptibility of questioning leads into the open space within which – *prior* to all beings, *prior* to the "gods" and their idols, *prior* to the human beings and their masks – it can then be decided what would be necessary in order to give rise to any kind of structure – with the goal of it being a blessing to beings and sanctified by beyng.

More originary and inceptual than any duty is steadfastness in the shrouding of beyng.

44. The Saga

The measure
The uncanny
The steadfastness [...]¹⁰
The errancy
The power
The word
The disconcertment
The patience

Measure:
Beyng is the measure for all human history and for all beings manifested within history, for beyng already determines why and how a measure is, and it determines how the "measure" is to be thought in terms of beyng.

Insofar as the human is μέτρον:
Measure – granting the measure
    Moderation
    For what and how – upon what ground?

How the measure gets lost in mediocrity.
To the extent that mediocrity belongs to the unconditioned domination of the machination (cf. Ponderings XIV, 40ff.).¹¹
    "Being the measure" – ἄνθρωπος – μέτρον
how that occurs and distinguishes the human being.
And what is at stake there;
to what end is which measure given in which sense.

---

¹⁰ *[Two abbreviations indecipherable].
¹¹ Martin Heidegger, *Ponderings VII–XI, Black Notebooks 1938–1939*, trans. Richard Rojcewicz (Bloomington: Indiana University Press, 2017).

How the human bestows the measure,
insofar as this bestowal of the measure distinguishes the essence of the human.

The human first measured is himself a measure for the human.

The human is taken measure of in his essence and is decided by beyng, and beyng bequeaths the human into the clearing of being and bequeaths the human himself. Will the human ever manage to take measure of this measuredness?

45. The Crux of the Error

They believe that everything concerned with "the fatherland" must be "political."

But "the fatherland" can only be approached and arrived at essentially if the fatherland itself is open to its essential ground. If the fatherland accomplishes that, then it has already become something essentially other than itself and everything political is the confinement of the fatherland into its corrupted essence.

In order to "approach" the fatherland, something must begin its journey from afar, and must have been underway for a long time, harboring the resolve for a long sojourn.

Wherever that fails to occur [*ereignet*], the fatherland is already shattered and it has been relinquished to a state of desolation due to its own errancy.

A people which builds upon its youth seems to be "young"; but it is neither old nor young, though it is certainly lacking the measure of its essence. For how would a tree ever manage to bear fruit and to come to its full mature essence if it only permitted the youth to have a say?

Those who are unripe and undiscriminating shatter the essence; and all youthfulness is nothing more than a way of reveling in mindlessness, especially when the youth still clings to the "old" in the emptiness of its ignorance, without ever having experienced maturity and ripeness, and it is presumptuous enough to assume that it is capable of interpreting the old.

Wherever the law of the plenitude of the essence is broken and bent, there the downfall has already begun, and there is no chance of turning it back.

46. Time-Space
(cf. Contributions, Grounding)[12]

At first time-space appears as a void sparsely populated by beings and yet incapable of being filled up.

Is this time-space itself not the fullness of the essential prevailing of the truth of beyng?

Why is it that thinking never overcomes this "emptiness?" Why is it that we so seldom experience the essential prevailing of the abyss and so seldom experience that which is not divine, neither human, nor lifeless, nor alive, while everything occurs before everything else – and yet it is not the absolute? Thoroughly alienated from beyng, we simply await everything from beings.

47. The Temporalization of Time

The temporalization of time is not a mere sequence, current, effluent of succession, nor an indeterminate "process," rather it is ecstatic through and through – encroaching *beyond* and yet holding *back* and it can only be thought from the essence of the essential prevailing of the event and the abyssal aspect of beyng.

The same goes for the unified clearing out of space.

48. Time-Space

"Time"
Time and space
Space and time
Place and now
The separation of the two –
the conjunction of the two.

Here everything is already in the emanating essence of "time," which is ecstatic-unified with "space" from a unity which can neither be thought as space, nor be thought as time.

Otherwise "time-space" just means a "segment" of "duration" within the "time-space" of, for example, "a year."

---

[12] Martin Heidegger, *Contributions to Philosophy (of the Event)*, trans. Richard Rojcewicz and Daniela Vallega-Neu (Bloomington: Indiana University Press, 2012).

Time-space is neither of the two, neither their sum, nor any other composite recently conjoined together. The time-space of what is already emanating – what happens as event in the event of appropriation (clearing).

The Word.
On the Essence of Language

(Outline of an Intimation)

The Quickening Element of the Word

The word quickens: it illuminates joyfully by signifying meaningly [*be-deutet*] the compliance into beyng (to the speaker).

Signification of meaning [*Be-deuten*]: it approaches through *hints* and leads into cover.

The radiance essences under cover.

The quickening cover.

The quickening element of the word is simultaneously the way in which the human *being* is granted a dwelling alongside beyngs [*Seyende*] as such – lodged covertly in the dwelling.

The Birth of Language

Beckon the heights to greet the depths.
Sow the seeds of the word from ahigh.
Carry up from the depths their ripeness for the saga.
Safeguard silence for the unspoken.
Build from it the dwelling of the human: language.
'Fore the human reigns his essence,
Calling to birth the pure dwelling,
Intimating the cradle of dwelling.

Language is the lone first dwelling of the human. Soil becomes arable, world fertile, earth bearing world, world first shields soil in the whiling expanse bestowed for the preservation of language.

Language houses the human by imparting to memory the manner of dwelling in the whiling expanse of the event of appropriation.

Expanse is the nurturing proximity of illuminated distance. The while is the preserving hesitation of the illuminating arrival. While and expanse are essentially the selfsame, unique and united in essence. That is the covert.

The covert is the cradle of the open, which illuminates itself to the enclosing gathering.

Keeping covert is sheltering happening as event. The appropriating movement of unconcealment (disclosing) and appropriating concealment (secreting) above all belongs to it.

Keeping covert grants the intimacy found between the expanse and the while, and only out of this intimacy does all time-space arise; its unity essences not only prior to any time and space, rather it still knows nothing of time as a sequence of nows and still knows nothing of space as the domain of extension of the corporeal.

The while is the pre-temporal appropriation of time.

The expanse is the pre-spatial appropriation of space.

The expanse nurtures, approaching, in hesitant preservation. The while preserves hesitantly in a nurturing approach.

The whiling expanse knows nothing of the empty uniformity of time and space. The limitation to the mere extension of the corporeal and of (temporal) succession is foreign to it as well.

The covert is the heart of the untimely pretemporal time-space. Covertly, the intimacy of the whiling expanse happens as event.

The covert is the essence of the heartfelt embrace. That is why the cradle of the open is also the heart of the enclosing. The cradling heart of the happening of the event hides the covert in its internal enclosure, concealing how the covert preserves the secret.

The core of the secret is that everything that happens as the event and within the event is the selfsame and that it finds its own property within the event. Everything proper to the event is the selfsame. The event is the unifying singularity, which is "one and all." If the saga dares to say the core of the secret, then it fails to illuminate the secret, but neither does the sage shroud the secret. Instead, the saga merely helps the secret to remain Itself in saying. Such assistance is originary guessing. The saga puzzles over the secret.

The expanse of the covert tarries in the secret. The secret disappropriates itself into the covert. But the covert is also the act of disappropriating through which the secret is first delivered to its property.

The property is grace, and grace is that within which the event remains with its own.

Grace is the benevolence of the secret. By granting itself together in the secret as the expanding while, grace remains – and grace alone remains – so covert in serenity. Everything beautiful is never anything more than the pale reflection of the serene.

The serene heals up the resplendent into the rift. This healing appropriates the hale purely, appropriating it as the expropriated one of all the selfsame directed into the unique element.

Yet how do resplendence and the rift enter into the healing of grace? They do not start out there. Instead they are their own property within the event, and they are brought to their property in the happening of the event. Grace seizes what is its own through disappropriation. The rift is found here, which first partitions off grace into benevolence so that grace in turn can be wrested away from its origin in the rift. Yet the rift partitions by first conjoining the open, which is proper to the secret of grace. The rift appropriates the conjoined rift of grace.

Grace grants its benevolence in the rift. The rift expropriates the grace of the secret so that the secret can be It itself on its own as the cradle of the covert. Through the separating-enjoining movement of disappropriation, the granted grace happens as event moving into serenity. The rift conjoins grace by separating (not dividing) grace and the serene. Within the scission, the intimacy of the whiling expanse moving into the secret happens as event.

The rift is the essence of anguish. Anguish essences in grace and remains essentially bound to the event. In its initial stage, this anguish is not the opposite of joy. Mourning is the opposite of joy. As essencing anguish, the rift is the illuminating-enjoining encounter with what blooms forth through the rift and arises from serenity as resplendence. That would cause resplendence to thoroughly dissolve itself without alienation [*Vereignung*] through the rift and to move into its own light, a light bereft of the juncture-rift, and in the process it would lose itself.

For this reason serenity essences in junction of this kind so that it can heal resplendence into the rift. Only the rift can heal. But the rift does not disappear because the forging rift is serene self-healing. Serene healing within the rift is the shrouding intimacy of the unique form of alienation [*Vereignens*].

The unique trait of all alienation [*Vereignens*] is healing into the rift. This healing is the origin of all the forms of unifying arising from the unity of the one, the one that is once again the only one.

The healing rift is the secret of grace.

The serenity of grace is the hale, within which all happening of the event as alienation [*Vereignen*] takes its rest.

Quiet is the hale property out of which the happening of the event – and along with it the essence of motion – is first apportioned to all motion.

For the forging of a way [*Be-wegen*] has its essence in the event of appropriation, which delivers to itself what is e-spied [*das Er-eigte*] in the happening of the event, beholding and discerning it, in order to grant it in such a way that it essences for itself as if it were its own [*in seinem Selbst selbig*].

This going back and forth in a discerning-granting movement has its unique form of stasis in motion, and there it has its "way." That is what the word "way" means: going back and forth. Motion [*Be-wegung*] is: being underway. This motion presents itself as the event of appropriation. Thinking – namely metaphysical thinking – otherwise defines motion in terms of the modification of a thing, of its location and point in time, or in terms of a change of condition. But why should motion [*Bewegung*] as the forging of a way [*Be-wegung*] be thought in terms of the way [*Weg*]? Why does thinking not follow the hint of the word?

What remains along the way [*auf dem Weg*] is underway [*unterwegs*]. Whatever goes that way is "away [*fort*]." It is gone [*weg*]. It whiles in the expanse of distance and preserves the arrival. The way [*Wëg*], however, essences in the scission, and the scission fits the rift from grace.

Motion rests in the rift. It is grounded in the rest of healing.

Rest is not the cessation of motion, rather it is the inception of motion, as long as inception is not meant to refer to a starting point [*Ausgang*]. Rest is the cradle [*Wiege*] in which all motion arises and sways. Motion is rooted in the rest of the cradle.

Only what cradles and has weight [*wiegt*] is capable of setting something into motion, namely the scale and weighing. Only what is adroit [*gewiegt*] can weigh [*wiegen*], have weight [*Gewicht haben*]. The human who is genuinely adroit moves about a great deal along all ways, he is familiar with these paths. Only the adroit human can weigh. Only he who has been weighed in the cradle is himself capable of weighing, and only he is permitted to take a risk.

The footpath is the intimate site of the motion of crossing hither and thither within the happening of the event. The footpaths provide a transition to motion (the way). Everything – cradle and way, footpath, scale and risk – arrives as the selfsame from the healing rest of grace.

The cradle shelters rest (the cradle keeps rest covered). The quiet element of the serene pacifies the movements of the happening of the event. Rest stills, yet rest does not eliminate motion. Rest calls the movements back into the cradle and thus imparts into it the junction-rift of its essence, thereby stilling the cradle. Rest is stillness only to the extent that rest – and only rest – nurses movements in a gesture that beckons back and has an impact.

Stillness is the beckoning call to return, which, in its greeting gesture, shows the way into the serene, and the serene enlists grace in the healing rift which favors the covert.

Intimation is the greeting-showing calling back of stillness. The stillness of grace intimating from the rift is the essence of the word.

The stillness of grace is the cradling womb of the event.

The human being is sown in this womb as its memory.

Sowing is letting something submerge into the serene stillness of the intimate cover, a cover leading to the upsurge in the blooming ripening of gratitude. This gratitude heals all commemoration into the sole element of the event.

Because the human being is sowed in the womb of grace in this way, while grace for its part is alienated to the healing scission moving into the encountering greeting issued both by the rift and resplendence, it is for this reason that the twofold commemoration is also apportioned to memory in accordance with the measure of duality of the whiling expanse, an expanse which originates from the covert of the secret.

The whiling expanse of the rift is depth.

The expanding while of resplendence is height.

Depth itself never goes under. A form of astonishment which produces a cloak of obscurity is proper to it. Through this cloak of obscurity, height illuminates itself into the inclining arrival of grace. In this astonishment, depth is elevated into lofty heights.

Height itself does not surge up. A form of illuminating evoking is proper to it, and through this evoking depth encloses itself into the distancing nearness of grace. In its evoking, height is sunken deep into the depths.

Depth astonishes height.

Height evokes depth.

Astonishment and evoking retrieve and deliver over what the healing stillness of grace once called out to them. They accomplish this by surpassing in the encountering greeting and by moving into the darkening of resplendence and into the illuminating of the rift. The festival of repetition appropriates itself in memory and is extracted out of the self-retrieval of astonishing depth and evoking height. This repetition remains essentially and eternally distinct from empty temporal succession as the preserving hesitation of the arrival (the while) is distinct from the sequence of nows (of time).

The healing up of the resplendent into the rift is the measure of the event resting in grace. Under this measure, memory is separated off harmoniously and portioned out to the intimacy of commemoration.

This commemoration encounters memory in a twofold state, for it arises both out of depth and out of height.

Being the memory of depth is the human essence of the steadfastly singular woman [*Weibes*].

Being the memory of height is the human essence of the steadfastly man.

The beginning can only come to be if the human being is sowed into the womb of the event.

The beginning is the event within memory. The festival only comes to be when the event tarries purely within the expanse of memory. This is the beginning: the fact that the grace of memory delivers itself into the ownership of the encountering greeting, arising from the astonishing depth of the rift and from the evoking height of resplendence.

The encountering greeting, however, can only appropriate itself if it prepares itself from time immemorial, preparing itself as the recipient of the greeting issued by the stillness of grace, and is thus ready to attend to the hint of the stillness of grace, in order to bring silence attentively close to the stilling rest. Consequently, the word finds itself in the answering-word [*Ant-wort*], which bequeaths the saga in the unspoken to itself.

Such an answering greeting to serenity, happening as event arising out of grace, receives the measure of the singular and enjoins itself to the healing force of the resplendence directed into the rift.

In the beginning, the greeting delivered over unfolds the twofold essence of commemoration, and this permits the essence of memory to be fulfilled in the festival.

In the beginning the unspoken arises out of the intimating stillness of anguishing grace and the human begins the saga leading to the birth of language.

The concealed intimacy of astonished depth and evoked height summons into the approaching proximity:

> Beckon the heights to greet the depths.
> Sow the seeds of the word from ahigh.
> Carry up from the depths its ripeness for the saga.
> Safeguard silence for the unspoken.
> Build from it the dwelling of the human: language.
> 'Fore the human reigns his essence,
> Calling to birth the pure dwelling,
> Intimating the cradle of dwelling.

When does the human learn to dwell upon this earth? He only learns it once it is called to his essence and has first of all learned to hear and to say that the sole dwelling place for his essence: language that is born in the word of the event.

But when does the human learn such a thing? He only learns it when he finds his way to memory in the event. This occurs when the event enters into memory in such a way that, through this very arrival, stillness – while serving as the mistress of all human life – teaches us to celebrate the presence of grace in the active silence of the unspoken. That occurs in the beginning. The beginning fits the twofold essence of the human being from the rift into salutary gratitude.

The greeting twofold of memory in the event essences in a manner that is infinitely distinct from both the species [*Geschlecht*] and its contrary within the domain of the living.

The grounding of the human conjoined into the saga of the word guiding into language essences in the beginning, long before the spawning of the human.

It is first of all necessary to learn to dwell within the appropriated human being. But how can dwelling be learned if the pure form of housing which already encompasses the human fails in advance to begin blossoming and fails to remain constant?

Plants and animals do not have language. They therefore remain sheltered in the species [*Geschlecht*]. Even thinking is only capable of initially indicating the essence of the species in terms of the event of appropriation.

Plants and animals remain in the species, for they "are" beyond the range of the beckoning stillness and are without the while of what once was, and yet they are not as memory. This being is life. It bears no lack within itself, for it is not capable of abstaining. Abstinence is only granted to commemorative thinking. The essential domain of the living is still closed off to thinking. Biology is the unconscious will to exclude thinking from this essential domain.

Biology is the metaphysics of the living. It thinks living things as the individuations of a genus. It thinks the genus-creating force of the species and the species itself in terms of the production of "individuals," and aims toward reproduction for the perpetuation of the species.

Metaphysics thinks the species as that which is sensible. To the extent that metaphysics represents the human as lifeform in a pre-emptive gesture, and to the extent that it is nonetheless obligated to acknowledge language as the characteristic essential property of the human, to that extent metaphysics transfigures the sensible into the supersensible of what is endowed with soul and spirit. Metaphysics in turn interprets soul and spirit in terms of that which is living.

Hence the thinking of metaphysics neither reaches into the originary level of the sensible, nor into the originary level of the supersensible, nor even to the origin of the distinction between the two.

Yet the originary element of the sensible is in no way depth. For the whiling expanse of the astonishing rift has already surpassed the sensible and, with it, its differentiation from the supersensible.

But the originary element of the supersensible is in no way the height. For the expanding while of evocative serenity has already surpassed the supersensible and, with it, its differentiation from the sensible.

More sensible than all sensibility of the living is the astonishing depth and hence this astonishing depth is more "sensible" than anything related to the drives.

More astounding than anything supersensible in the human spirit is the evocative height, and hence the evocative height is "more spiritual" than all spirit.

Yet the distinction between, on the one hand, high depth and deep height, and on the other hand, sensible and supersensible is not one of degree in the same domain of gradation. The distinction involves the domains themselves and is grounded in the essential diversity of being and the essential diversity of the event.

Hence language is essentially and infinitely distinct from what metaphysics knows when it combines the words together, forging it out of the sensible body of sound and the supersensible spiritual element of the meaning of the word.

And yet:

The riddle of life and the secret of language rest simply in separation in the same cradle of beyng, which thinking now calls the event. Everything proper to the event is the selfsame. The unifying unity of the unique is the riddle of all riddles.

Everything essencing from the event is the selfsame. Though it is granted a name early on and still remains unrecognized in its concealed appropriation, the Ἕν shines.

The selfsame essences unified as the sole element. In order to think this, it would be necessary to experience everything simply as the selfsame from the intact grace of the healing rift. The rift grants simple conjoining.

If one were to think everything as the selfsame, that would easily create the illusion that such thinking hardly needs to be attended to at all, under the mistaken impression that the only thing that is proper to thinking is the thoughtless mashing up of everything together. But the mere negligence which permits all borders and structures to remain mixed up with one another would be enough to give rise to this confusion.

Yet the simple element of the selfsame appropriates itself from the wealth of the juncture. Its conjoining, however, knows nothing of the playful play with contraries.

The representation initially evoked by the saga, when it is understood as a proposition, may at first appear to be nothing more than the mere positing of contraries and a game of sublating these contraries. Yet that very representation is the opposition arising from the event.

This opposition is not suspended in the represented unity of contraries, for the unity of the sole element remains bound to the event, with the result that the unity of all opposition and the that which opposes itself are never limited to a duality which purportedly has a unity hovering above it as a third distinct element.

Everything that opposes has once been surpassed in what is proper to the event, within which everything is the selfsame.

If thinking experiences everything as the selfsame, then everything that has been thought returns back to itself and shows itself in the constant cycle of return of the one to the other. This creates the new impression that thinking is moving around in a circle. But that impression is apparently in error, for customary thinking and opining actually show everything by way of a proof, which presses forwards without returning, neglecting the movement from the one to the other.

Yet the semblance of the circular movement is the genuine sign, or can at least be a sign that, within the ring of beyng, thinking has found its way as a footpath leading to the event. It is first necessary to think the sameness of the selfsame and the selfsame of the selfhood of the self in terms of the event, for the event conceals within itself the covertness of the healing unification from the unity of the uniqueness of grace.

Thinking everything as the selfsame is the most difficult form of thinking. The weight of this task of thinking is even heavier than precious metals and gold. For this task of thinking originates from the cradle of beyng and constantly arcs back toward the secret.

The treasure bearing the heft apportioned from the cradle introduces the slow pace of the footpaths into thinking. Yet a form of play holds sway in the weighing of the cradle and in the weight of the scale. This play is the intimation of the beautiful, which rests in serenity.

The language unique to the saga remains in the unspoken. It can never be uttered immediately in the habitual everyday realm, nor can it be used to facilitate communication.

Unspoken, it is nothing more than the attribution and saying of the conversation in its beginning phases. The saga of the unspoken is not a form of verbal utterance which describes something objective. The saga is the memory of what is to be said itself.

Only slowly does the mantra introduce the language of the habitual everyday realm to the care for speaking by drawing it from the conversation in its beginning phases. The structure and flow of the care for speaking both originate from the concealed junction of the event.

> Follow in saying the hints of the word.
> Avoid interpreting the wordless vocabulary.

The form of thinking which emerges from memory as the essence of the human experiences its way while underway upon the footpaths.

Thinking is astonished by the astonishing depth. That is why thinking evokes everything proper to the event as the selfsame, while everything is weighed in the weighing and cradling womb of grace and weighed in the attentive vigilance of the guardians.

> Keep silent in the word.
> Thus language grounds.

The Beginning

By attending to the hint of the word, thinking thinks the word in this way:

The beginning is the event in memory. Yet being memory in the event is the essence of the human. The beginning is essential to the human being, but not merely to the human being as something human.

Beckoned humans are permitted to belong to and listen into the beginning. But the beginning does not belong to the human.

Ginnen, ginnan – ancient is the word and it means: to break, to break apart (bread), to relish it, to avail oneself of it; to use it (*frui*).

The reference to the rift and to what grants itself is contained within *ginnan* if this is thought as using up by breaking apart, which in being used inclines toward what is being used and, in taking it what is used, elevating it to its united essence.

The be-ginning "gin-s [*ginnt*]" by be-ginning [*be-ginnt*]. In the beginning the event makes use of the human being essentially.

"To consume" originally means: to make use of something. The way in which the event makes use of, the way in which it uses (and never mis-uses) the human being, is nonetheless to be thought from the standpoint of the event. The event be-gins in appropriation and it *is* the beginning by weighing the human being as the twofold commemoration in the compliance to the stillness of grace. The lulling element of the beginning is appropriating consumption. Since the human being is made use of in this way, beyng needs (it has the need for) to use the human being. For us the word "to consume" has been worn out in everyday use. Hence, we are only capable of thinking the pure essence of intimately appropriating consumption slowly and with effort.

The Unique Element

The word names the event as the preserving truth [*Wahr-heit*] of beyng. In this truth beyng unveils itself and remains sheltered in its essential (appropriating) reference to the human being as memory within the event. Beyng is only beyng as the appropriation of the human being to the memory of the happening of the event of beyng itself directed into truth.

In billowing forth from the cradle of grace, appropriation is the preserving unification. In this unification, the peculiar uniqueness of everything proper within the event has its oneness of unity with everything that is its own.

The one of *all* that is proper to it and the unity excluding nothing, the event, does not come to be as the segregated one of grace, rather as the alienated one, as the sole element preserving all.

The event is the sole element al-one [*all-ein*]; it is the only sole element, and it harbors the originary unity of oneness. The sole element alone is never that which excludes and is hence never exclusive. It is that which is inclusive, yet it is not inclusive as a later supplement, rather in its own originary execution. The sole element arises from the curing grace whose intact dimension heals the illuminating quickening and heals everything illuminated within the quickening into the rift.

The unity singularizing and unifying all of the sole element is only capable of uniting into one unity if it manages to requisition everything proper to it into its property. The sole element knows neither excluding nor separation, nor does it even know the process of uniformization which eradicates all that is properly its own. Moreover, both this separation and uniformization are essentially subsequent additions, for they never originate from appropriation.

The sole unique element is never "only the one," while it expels the other as mere remainder.

Yet at the same time the sole element is exclusive in an essential sense; namely, in such a way that, in its expansive whiling, it cannot let anything at all essence, from which it would then be capable of distinguishing itself.

Hence, for the sole element alone only commemoration is decisive. Beginning from its very source, it has already escaped being bound to rigid distinctions without origins. Having eluded those distinctions from the beginning, it simply never devolves into the willful positing of oppositions.

Since it is struck by grace alone, this de-cided commemoration is the sole memory within the event. It is the concealed source of the freedom of the human being. Articulated under the name of "the unique element," the event readily encounters us again and again as something objective. The event thus seems to exist as something set apart, similar to the names spoken in the vocabulary words of language, which as spoken words and words that can only be heard in that way, never name anything; that is to say, they never bear the originary words to saying through their answering. Mere words appear in such a barren state as a result of how they were ejected from the domain of the pliant answer which responds to the word. Yet if language as a whole only encounters us as an inventory of vocabulary words held together in a network of grammatical rules, then language appears to us solely as the expression of human linguistic tools. Language conceived in this way is thus an organ of the human and is consequently dependent upon the organism, which is regarded as the essential space for the lifeform "human" in the biological representation of the organism. If it can consequently be dislodged from this "organic" captivity, then language no longer belongs anywhere. Language itself is homeless [*heimatlos*]. Language, which in truth will actually remain the first stable housing for the human being. Yet language remains a stable housing only if it is appropriated in the expansive while and only if it dwells under the cover in which the word moves toward the answer.

How are we ever supposed to hear the word in this name, or to hear its saying power, if we only hear the name of "the unique element" as one among many words constituting a vocabulary? How are we supposed to hear it if we have no intimation of the essence of language?

The unique element, which is commemoration alienated in the beginning to its sole gratitude, has its origin arising from the unique element of grace.

This heritage arises from what once was. The heritage is the oldest and is never surpassed in its origin. That which the oldest origin is permitted to possess from the unique element is the sole form of nobility. "Noble [*Edel*]" here means: bearing the sole origin solely in the disposition [*Gemüt*]. Yet the disposition is the bloom of memory.

The lone commemorators are those who bear the noble disposition [*Edelmütigen*]; for the noble disposition [*Edelmut*] is the blooming forth of the blossom.

Blossoming is the graceful self-illumination of the beauty of ripening into the sole fruit that has been. Yet this fruit is the unspoken language born in the beginning. The noble disposition is the memory of healing unity preserving within itself, and this is a unity which rests in the unifying oneness of the unique element.

The event is the weighing unification arising from the sole element, and the event itself its uniqueness.

Addenda

The Different Manners and Grades of Silence

in reference to grace, stillness, word, saga, the unspoken, the spoken.
Silence and memory.
(still commemoration),
speechless *astonishment*,
attentive memory,
the word surpassing,
inquiring back into the bequest.

*

The Word

is the stillness of grace intimating from anguish.

grace
stillness
intimating
anguish
intimating stillness
intimating from anguish

Why – in the downfall – is the saga of the unspoken now necessary for the preparation of language from the word?

intimation and the arrival
of return
event

Anguish and stillness; why not likewise joy?

(event) requisitioning	*anguish*: time-space
grace	of *intimation*
	stillness stills time-space
anguish	anguish – *rift* – outline
	resplendence
stillness	
the word	Language as wresting,
(event) memory	bearing the word forth
the answer memory:	from the rift into *resonance*.
the saga	commemoration
the *un*spoken ↕	re-saying (poetry)
speaking	re-minding (thinking)
language	pre-saying
the spoken word	reciting together
language as the shrine of the	reciting with one another
word	the conversation
	articulation
	speaking
	language

Downfall into Concealed Language

The nobility of the downfall is only proper to that which is concealed in the originary upsurge. Everything else simply perishes in desolation.

*

Language: The Dwelling Place of the Human Being

Preparing language from the word
through the saga in the unspoken.
How memory as the essence of the human
permits the historical human to dwell in language.
Dwelling in language
and interpretation.
Articulation – language – interpretation

*

Language Wrests

the word – from stillness.
Language extracts the word from the rift and bears it forth into reso-
nance and the voice.

*

Stillness

slaking thirst – *soothing the tears.*
Stilling from stillness; stillness alone stills. But what is *stilling*?
(What does it still?) Or stilling (intransitive) but through (event)!
Still – "quiet" – harboring quiet, and thus bestowing
"*quiet*" – gathering of motion in the downfall of its upsurge.
"Quiet": not loud – "Be quiet!" – against noise
Stillness – quiet – gathering – *tarrying* – time-space –
sheltering
Referring everywhere to the word, but not yet breaking,
rather intimation.
Sheltering and intimation – (event)
Meaning – bequest
stilling in the event – *memory*
showing and calling back, beckoning showing.
Calling as surpassing, catching up, repeating.
Not the *soundless*! Volume and noise are not the call.
Beckoning showing – *vocation*, calling up, naming, appointing,
determining, destinal sending [*Ge-schick*].
Stillness, style, junction, impression.

Stillness –
1. not privative
2. hence not un-determined; ὕλη
3. *calling* and memory – memory and attending.

*

Stillness

silence in the beginning,
stilled originarily in the beginning out of stillness,
the *fore-word.*

*

Stillness

Departure (of the gods):
no new god,
for no god at all,
for holier and the holy first hale.
Not anthropomorphism,
not atheism,
not indifference.

The Lightweighted

rooted in the weighty.
Not by taking things lightly do we withstand
the lightweighted and playful,
rather out of weightiness we bear the hefty and slow.

*

Listening and Memory
(cf. Summer Semester '44)[13]

Listening – word

Call: listening –
   – as acoustic perception of sounds
   – as attentive self-conjoining to what is to be said to us, the attentive
   self-conjoining authentic precisely in *silence* without sound.
   Silence even as what is "still," keeping in place – being attentive (be
   still, so that we can perceive something, not necessarily something
   audible), rather what which proclaims itself in reflection.
"Listening" –

*

[13] Martin Heidegger, *Heraclitus: The Inception of Occidental Thinking and
Logic: Heraclitus's Doctrine of the Logos*, trans. Julia Goesser Assaiante and
S. Montgomery Ewegen (London: Bloomsbury Academic, 2018).

The Unspoken
(cf. Hölderlin's "Germania")[14]

can only be the word which beckons to language.

How *is* the unspoken itself to be if it is supposed to grant a dwelling?

Unspoken is the word.

Unspoken too is language.

Each in its own way, so that the unspoken dimension of the word yields for itself the unspoken dimension of language.

How do we dwell in the unspoken?

The mere act of not speaking out does not yet preserve the unspoken – or it no longer does.

The unspoken and interpretation.

Interpretation and dwelling in language.

The unspoken is not the consequence and result of silence, rather it is the bequest (overcoming and destiny) of stillness.

*

The Word

The event

the word – intimating stillness

the appropriated word: the answering word

the answering word as saga. Echo – in echoing back the word first tolls.

The saga as conversation

conversation and the preparation of language.

The saga is the *unspoken*.

The unspoken prepares itself for language in "conversation";

"conversation" as word and answer

encountering bound to the event

conversation and language; the "spoken"

enunciation and the spoken.

*

---

[14] Martin Heidegger, *Hölderlin's Hymns "Germania" and "The Rhine,"* trans. Julia Ireland and William McNeill (Bloomington: Indiana University Press, 2014).

The Word
(cf. "the unspoken" in Hölderlin's "Germania")[15]

The "word" "is" the stillness of grace arising within the event and inti-mating from anguish. This stillness (appropriated) re-instills in silence, and silence encounters stillness as gratitude, arising from the encounter of the appropriating region and as the encountering reaching to the word. This encountering is the proper answer to this word.

The appropriated encountering of silence directed to stillness issues as the "echo" of stillness and of the word.

"Echo" is the appropriating encountering as re-petition, and it is the originary re-petition.

We only know the "echo" from its sound and tone – from its rever-beration. Yet in the originary essence of the word, we are not permitted to begin with the sonic element of the spoken; we also cannot think that stillness is in relation to the sonic, hence we cannot think the con-trast of the non-sensible in relation to the sensible.

The distinction between the sensible and non-sensible (supersensi-ble) is a metaphysical distinction. Stillness is essentially bound to the event, it is "more sensible" than the sensibility pertaining the mere senses, and it is more perceptible – by virtue of appropriating more thoroughly – than black and white. Stillness, moreover, is more "affec-tive" than sense impressions are. Everything that is impressionable is still thought in an objective matter, and remains at the most external and superficial level.

The *approach* as event of appropriation is not only more originary in terms of degree, rather it is also more originary in its essence and in terms of the truth of beyng.

*

The Word

The word "is" – stillness of grace intimating within the event out of anguish. (Cf. "the unspoken" in Hölderlin, "Germania.")

The event appropriates (permits to "essence") the answering word. The word is intimating stillness.

[15] See previous footnote.

The answer is appropriated, it is memory which silently perceives stillness, and it is reflective *gratitude* – encountering. It is the appropriated memory remaining in what is its own as it originates from commemoration, i.e. the encountering of gratitude.

*

Re-Turning Thinking

The impression created by extrapolating from the mere meanings of words

(e.g. event – truth,

beginning – consuming).

1. In what way does this impression remain?
2. Why does it come to that?

    Estrangement [Entfremdung] from the word, the *violence* of the "*actual.*"

    Forgetting of being – abandonment by being.
3. The inhuman in the human,

    the *failure in the face of the word*

    no ability to dwell in stillness

    τέχνη and the encroachment of beings on being

    τέχνη – εἶδος – ἰδέα.

*

Whoever believes he has reached his goal turns back

The sound which lets stillness toll and does not even perceive itself. The sounding which only makes noise (hears itself), which only has an ear for itself.

How stillness stills: it is stilled down by stillness and brought into silence by stillness; it is not yet a sounding, rather it is originary and only then can it be elevated into sound.

Silence as thanking – thinking and poetizing.

Word – Sign – Conversation – Language

I. THE WORD AND LANGUAGE

The Sign
(cf. Summer Semester 1939, The Word and Language)[16]

1. The Word

Even now we hardly have any intimation of how originally the word bears and safeguards history. We know almost nothing of the word's concealed references.

The human has long sought out the word only in terms of discourse. As mere talking, discourse once again falls short when placed in contrast to action, which is recognized based on its outcome. In its spoken form, the word becomes a technical vehicle for the will and no longer counts for anything when the will is subsumed into the outcome.

Even if the word as a construct of language is judged and cultivated "artistically," that changes nothing about its fixed metaphysical-technical essence. This remains the case insofar as metaphysics obscures the essence of the word and displaces both the way leading to the essence of the word and obscures the essential experience of the word; this is the modern metaphysical essence of language in its entirety.

Cf. On Logos in Heraclitus and Summer Semester 1944.[17]

---

[16] Martin Heidegger, *On the Essence of Language: The Metaphysics of Language and the Essencing of the Word Concerning Herder's Treatise On the Origin of Language*, trans. Wanda Gregory Torres and Yvonne Unna (Albany, NY: SUNY Press, 2004).

[17] Martin Heidegger, *Heraclitus: The Inception of Occidental Thinking and Logic: Heraclitus's Doctrine of the Logos*, trans. Julia Goesser Assaiante and S. Montgomery Ewegen (London: Bloomsbury Academic, 2018).

2. Language – Word

Word and tuning of beyng
Tuning (resplendence) the play without noise
for reflection – the signification of meaning [*Be-deuten*]
as the play of happening of the event into the
sign.

3. Word as Language

And language brought into the framework of the system of signs.
Sign itself – formally objective, representation in the mode of a thing
The essence of language thus strangled
even if the occasional moments
could be captured
by flattening out this framework.
Language – word – truth – beyng.

4. The Way along the Footpaths (Variations)[18,19]

The truth of beyng is the event.

The event, which conceals itself for its own sake, is the self-concealing essence of the inception. The inception is the simple element of beyng. The simple is the fact that beyng essences and nothing is granted in the process. "Beings" arise up into this and never "out of" it. In the midst of all of this, thinking always says *the selfsame*, for thinking only says the simple and only says it in advance.

The sole and characteristic element of steadfast thinking concerns how it fits itself into tarrying in the selfsame, while it refuses to explain being in terms of other beings – even if it is dealing with the highest being = that which is most in being [*Seiendste*].

---

[18] Part of Volume 72.

[19] {TN: In the Contents, this section is titled "The Way of the Saga (Variations)" [*Der Weg der Sage* (Variationen)]. In the body of the text the title is "The Way along the Footpaths (Variations)" [*Der Weg der Stege (Variationen)*]. I have left the two titles in accordance with the original.}

5. The Word and the Event

We only experience how being bequeaths itself in the word once we have thought the word in a manner bound to the event. Integral to thinking in that way is the inconspicuous poetry, thinking and remembrance. This remembrance does not even need to be commemorated.

The errant illusion that being is first produced by the word and is merely stamped upon the buzz of impressions is an illusion that could only arise once the word has been transformed into a proposition, while the proposition in turn has been transformed to a judgment, and judgment in turn transformed to a representation – a representation within which the subject objectifies an object. Even at this point there is still the possibility of attributing a "creative" meaning to poetry, but at the same time there also lurks the danger of overburdening language in its essence by confining it within the sphere of subjectivity. This results in a suspicion regarding the word and the dominance of an arbitrariness in the use of vocabulary.

The event-bound essence of the word delivers the clearing into which the appropriated element (beings) arises. It occurs in such a way that beings are first bequeathed to their own property and then announces the departure word which stands in contrast to the word. Language is the answer to the word.

6. Thinking and Poetizing – The Word

The preparation [?][20] of the word of language.
The word of beyng – the inceptual word.
The word of language as the *word* bequeathed, which must find itself in the structure of vocabulary words.
Language not "expression," rather history itself – responsibility.
Because *poetizing and thinking* refer to *the primordial beginning of the inception and* hence refer to the human (history – Da-sein – "dwelling" – being-in-the-world), they are therefore inceptually opposed [?][21] to the word of beyng and the word of language is therefore *not expression*.
The language of the poet,
the saying of the thinker.
Responsibility and handing over.

[20] {TN: included in the original.}
[21] {TN: included in the original.}

7. The Word – Signification – "Signs"

We take everything to be an object by representing it in an objective-technical manner, and this even includes the word in the form of vocabulary. We then encounter objects which are named with words (vocabulary). The speaking human produces the vocabulary and applies it to objects in order to signify them and to make them identifiable by means of signs. Once "the word" has been unleashed from the unchecked [?][22] domain of objectification, then even the most deep-minded "philosophy of language" will no longer be able to help us out of this error, for even language itself speaks this error when it depicts its findings about the word as language.

Regarded from the perspective of the history of beyng, however, we experience that we do not apply the word as vocabulary like a tool applied to objects, rather in the originary non-objective word we first perceive not only objects, but we also perceive all beings as such. *Where* then is "the word" located if it does not adhere to the thing as a human product? The metaphysics of language, which is based on the misrecognition of the essence of the word, neither inquires into this "where," nor is it capable of defining the "where." Metaphysics instead hastily retreats back to the speaking human, if, that is, the question even manages to come into contact with metaphysics. If beings first encounter us in the word as the word – or perhaps in the "word" that is not yet found – and if beings are only suitable to beings in being, then the word must belong to being itself, and it may only be inquired into from the standpoint of the truth of beyng.

All "philosophy of language" has been overcome with this step.

Yet the word is also released from its confinement to *wording* [Wort*laut*]. It is not as if "mere meaning" is now what is left behind. For with the wording of vocabulary [*Wörterlaut*], meaning also becomes irrelevant and so too does differentiation as *the* first guiding thread of the analysis of language. The pure word is in no way the "meaning," for meaning only constitutes the objectification of the referent [*Gemeinten*] in opining [*meinenden*] representation. The word does not "have meaning" and meaning does not show, rather the word is the clearing of being itself. The clearing is first made use of unwittingly [?][23] by the "meaning" of beings and "signs" intended for beings.

---

[22] {TN: included in the original.}
[23] {TN: included in the original.}

Yet the essential fold [?][24] of the word also conceals itself here. The word of thinking is essentially distinct from the word of poetry.

To what extent? Why does precisely this differentiation happen as event? The essence decides for itself in the reference of the word to the human, and the division into thinking and poetry is decided along with it.

8. The Word

Are words just vocabulary and vocabulary merely the trawling nets cast out to capture thoughts? What are thoughts without remembrance of the unsaid and the unsayable [*Unsägliche*]? How would the unsaid ever be able to remain within what it is if the saying does not bear what it has said as if it were on an offering plate?

Admittedly, that is a different way of thinking the necessity of the otherwise unnecessary and bothersome word, which is prone to leading us astray.

The word is the quiet voice of the greeting. In greeting tenderness reigns.

9. Language and Word

Neither practicing discipline in speaking, nor the cultivation of writing – were anyone to attempt such a thing these days – would be capable of rescuing language from its desolation.

The transformation must originate from the origin of language. The origin is concealed in the word. But the word happens as event only after beyng bequeaths its truth to humans and after human beings have learned how to protect this truth by standing steadfast within the truth.

The calamity which has been thrust upon orality and writing can only be broken by first overcoming the forgetting of being. This overcoming can only happen as beyng-historical event.

---

[24] {TN: included in the original.}

10. The Word and the Sign

If ἀληθεύειν is only a form of σημαίνειν in the manner of ἀπόφανσις, then φαίνεσθαι and ἀλήθεια are related to one another essentially.
τὰ φανερώτατα – τὰ ἀληθέστατα – ἡ ἀλήθεια – τὸ ὄν ᾗ ὄν – ἀλήθεια – οὐσία
Parmenides: τὸ γὰρ αὐτό
The relation of σημαίνειν (*to make it known – in which sense?*) and ἀληθεύειν?
1. where λόγος: here σημαίνειν is the more originary.
    But what is the relation?
    Is ἀληθεύειν a form of σημαίνειν and what does the specific difference involve –
    or [is] the relation otherwise?
2. if σημαίνειν itself is intended in a more inceptual sense – *illuminating* – guiding – not mere display of what is present, arising as such.

11. Origin of the Word and Discourse (Aristotle) *De Interpretatione*, ca. 2ff.

κατὰ συνθήκην
ὅταν γένηται σύμβολον σῆμα (σύνθημα)
stated absolutely or like ὄνομα
σύμβολον (not σῆμα) or yet is it so?
Rather σύμβολον is supposed to indicate the condition under which σημαίνειν of the ὄνομα is possible.
    The contrary to φύσει is θέσει; θέσις in σύνθημα.
σύνθημα (θῆμα – σῆμα!)
agreement – appointment – *con-cor-dance* [Über-ein-kunft] –
the "watchword" – word appointed [*verabredete*] – sign appointed.
Is all discourse essentially ap-point-ment [*Ver-ab-redung*]?
How is it formed and what is it based upon?
What makes it necessary?
In taking recourse to ap-point-ment [*Ver-ab-redung*], is speech not referred back to "talking [*Redung*]?" Who comes to an agreement with whom and how do they do so in advance?
Or is "concordance" merely an unsuitable explanation for speech and the word, beginning with the fact that individually arising humans express themselves in sounds and understand one another "in the process?"

12. The Word and the Hand

Because beyng is on the lookout for its essential prevailing, it shies away from its own clearing. The inceptual ground of beyng is therefore this lookout as preservation. The grounding of this preservation is bound to the inception and offers to us the initial indication of the essence of preserving truth [*Wahr-heit*].

Truth as preservation is the concealment preserving the inception inceptually. The inception arises from the necessity for reticence, and the word and its rare form originate from this reticence.

Yet the essentially preserving word is first safeguarded in the sign as the signified showing element which reveals itself. This word, in turn, nonetheless shows itself in the clearing of the saga and shows itself as [?][25] word.

The hand and showing and sketching.

II. THE SIGN

(ITS ESSENCE BOUND TO THE EVENT)

13. Happening as Event

Happening as event
    favor   turn
    gratitude
the origin of signs bound to the event
signs and *turning clearing-concealment*

14. Event-Bound Essence of Signs

is based on the fact that signs are the footpaths of the inception.
But what are footpaths?
footpaths and event
cf. Variations III[26]

---

[25] {TN: included in the original.}
[26] Part of Volume 72.

15. The Showing of Signs

If we think it in a manner bound to the event, then showing is not only the juncture of unconcealing and concealing, rather showing appropriates itself only in the inceptual form of self-showing showing. It does so in such a way that showing is the illuminating-surpassing sheltering of the inception directed into the departure as the inceptual moment. This sheltering appropriates within itself the affinity as the open homeland of the truth of beyng, emerging within beings themselves as what is appropriating.

In contrast, the merely metaphysical delimitation of the essence of signs unwittingly restricts itself to the sign-things which happen to be at hand. The sign is sign for ... and signifies. The essence of showing remains undetermined or, in contrast, it is only comprehended as a form of representation, as pre-signification, as pro-curing for representation and as interpretation. The movement of concealment remains unnoticed and, therefore, the movement of unconcealment also receives no satisfactory definition. No wonder then that, above all, the unity of both concealment and unconcealment, but especially the origin of this unity, remains unthought. The drivel produced about the symbol [*Symbol*] is characteristic of the arbitrary and superficial nature of the metaphysical delimitation of the essence of the sign.

At most, the definition of the sign remains at the level of showing as the act of pointing something out [*Auf-etwas-weisen*] and representing it. While, in accordance with the manifold interpretations of representation, different versions of the "sign" also arise; for example, the sign can be understood as pointing out something, or as summoning the representation of something (in consciousness) within the soul; psychology is at work here, i.e. metaphysics.

Otherwise the sign is immediately understood based on the meaning of "signification," while the nature of showing as depicting also remains unclear here (*notare, insignare, designare*) ("they generally indicated [*bezeichnet*] that x was the culprit").

depicting – furnishing with a sign, equipping, making identifiable through the sign – for example, trees in the woods which are designated to be cut down.

16. Sign

Play – prelude – initial sounding
and sign

The self-showing as the tolling of the inconspicuous-soundless voice of the word of the claim.

17. The Showing of Signs

In order to show that which it is tasked with showing [*sein zu Zeigendes*], the sign must show itself, but it must show itself in such a way that it passes by itself and, in passing by, it indicates. The unity of showing is to be sought in this movement of passing by, although showing as self-showing and showing beholden to the sign are different varieties of showing.

18. Sign

Originary showing bound to the event does not "signify" anything.
Insofar as the sign is established as signification, in that case only *one* essential moment is taken in a one-sided and external way as the only possibility, and the alethetic sheltering essence of the sign is not recognized. The sign bound to the event as movement of *beyng* – not the movement of beings.
Hence the distinction between natural and produced signs has no bearing at all and is itself a merely derivative distinction.

Sign as signification – this characterization lends the sign a one-sided character of representation and positing; it only attends to *unconcealment* and *delivering*. This accounts for the common perplexity surrounding the concept of the "symbol," about which a fair amount of drivel is making the rounds.

19. The Essence of the Sign as σῆμα

is θῆμα – σύνθημα
Initially that refers to something *posited*, which is standing ready, something which *stands* for another, something *for* something else, instead of for itself.

Simultaneously, there is a form of concordance within it.

20. Sign – συνθήκη

Con-cordance
coming together as one with one another.

Coming to what? This involves coming to a point at which showing itself in its showing gives the initial jolt to the ones who are coming and puts them down the right path.

The originally unifying element of the one, *about which* there is then accord.

Sign – *showing*.

Signification as something distinct from inceptual showing, likewise *meaning* as something distinct.

21. Signs and Footpaths

Steadfast thinking about signs is commemoration of the concealed essence of signs, which is bound to the event. Steadfast thinking does not aim at the elaboration of a theory of signs and is not interested in the application of such a theory.

Steadfast thinking only instructs on how to attend to the inceptual signs and how to stand within the signs and how to follow them along their track.

These signs are the footpaths. Yet, given that it is inevitable that thinking must begin with the metaphysical mode of thinking, it is necessary to mention a few things about signs in order to facilitate communication. We should not be misled into expecting a theory of signs. Yet perhaps the perplexity and superficiality which is dominant in all metaphysics, especially with regard to the definition of the system of signs, stems from the same source as metaphysics itself: from the forgetting of being. But perhaps we cannot follow the overcoming of this forgetting in any other way, but can only do so by being ready to stand within the signs bound to the event.

22. The Fundamental Trait of all Signs Bound to the Event

Their fundamental trait is based on overcoming. Beyng (differentiation) is what shows itself, and that which is showing in self-showing is the truth of beyng. Everything happens as event in the event.

Does the sign bound to the event lack anything at all which is perceptible to the senses, i.e. anything bound to the earth in a beyng-historical manner? No – but this earth-bound element is, in each case, first glimpsed in the sign and never posited as an object, which in turn first assumes the task of showing. But the earth – belonging to the homeland as the happenings of the event [*die Ereignete*] – seals off the event of signs. The indeterminate aspect of the sign bound to the event, that which is non-objective in the customary sense, is precisely what is bound to the earth, and is precisely what has happened in the event – "beings" in terms of known actuality. Nonetheless, this in-between is purified in the simplicity and poverty of what happens in the event, which has managed to escape the expansionist raids carried out by "technology."

23. Showing – Inceptual – Signs and Footpaths

Not merely making comprehensible,
also not ἀληθεύειν displaying what is present,
rather concealing in illumination, *guiding into overcoming.*
Footpaths – are signs,
but are all signs footpaths?

24. The Beyng-Historical Essence of Signs

The beyng-historical essence of signs is to be thought as *bound to the event*.

Showing as self-showing – illuminating self-concealment of the truth of beyng.

This essence of signs is incomprehensible in terms of objective-metaphysical explanation and in terms of the initiation of signs as things (signals and symbols), even if the entirety of the metaphysical system of signs has its concealed origin in the beyng-historical realm.

"Signs" are not objects which appear to us, nor are they something which is utilized in the service of representation, production or establishment.

Signs happen as event [*er-eignen*] – they guide, they bring, they tune.

How is the distinction between *footpaths and signs* to be determined?

Is the selfsame thought within that distinction? To what extent are both footpaths and signs necessary?

25. "Signs" and Showing

The manner, extent, and justification for the interpretation of the essence of the "sign" depends upon how "showing" is experienced and is understood, but it also depends upon which modes of showing are unwittingly posited as decisive and subsequently get formalized.

The showing of the signifying thing (tool of signification) is only scantly elucidated in "Being and Time." This special form of showing has its essence in the showing bound to the event, and this showing conceals itself in the truth of beyng.

26. Signs

Happening as event as the guiding of footpaths.
Guiding – as bringing in the act of showing,
bringing showing.

27. In the Sign Of
(cf. Variations)[27]

Being greeted, conjoining to the hints, thinking attentively.
The showing of signs is forging intimation and illuminating greeting.
Showing essences in illuminating concealment, and this concealment conceals the departure.

28. The Alethetic Essence of the Sign

"Sign" and being there [*Da sein*] –
that is the showing happening as event as shining illumination and conjoining.
Conjoining.
"Sign" and "world" –
that is the unity of the connection of relations of reference (according to *Being and Time*).
"Sign" and overcoming
"Sign" and word

[27.] Part of Volume 72.

The originary word is a form of showing bound to the event.

But the word cannot be thought in terms of vocabulary words, for vocabulary words are initially regarded as sounds and writing, while sounds and writing in turn serve as signals.

29. Standing in the Sign Of

Here that means the steadfast essence of the inception bound to the event. It means that the inception "stands" within the signs which we call the footpaths and that, at the same time, it – having been appropriated by the human essence – stands within the showing self-showing of signs. The clearing of beyng appropriates itself as this self-showing. This "standing" of the inception conveys that it "rests" in a manner bound to the event in the clearing-concealing essence (departure) and that it is "persistent," without this "persistence" being thought in terms of mere duration or in terms of the mere presence of something.

This "standing" of the human being says that the human conjoins himself into the safeguarding of the clearing of beyng. There he corresponds to the "standing" of the inception as that which the inception requires.

30. Sign

By showing itself, the sign yields forth what is to be shown.
In each case a concealing is unveiled.

While it immediately captures the next thing, it only slowly begins to sense the Other.

Showing here is *alethic* and this showing is more inceptually as *unconcealing concealing* – bound to the event.

What is shown is not "meaning," "sign," nor "symbol" – however one might interpret a symbol, whether as "signal" or "cypher."

31. How the Event is Bound to the Sign, How the Sign is Bound to the Event

The event bequeaths the clearing (the locale, homes [?]).[28]

---

[28] {TN: included in the original.}

The event appropriates overcoming (the simple, the inception).

This only essential consequence for the sign that is initially visible is that the sign unconceals, conceals, and disconceals not merely itself alone (that which shows itself), but also what it shows; it conceals itself not only as what is to be shown, but also as [what is] showing.

32. Signs and the Event

Signs are essential to the event in an inceptual sense.

They show themselves and, by showing themselves, they show the way into overcoming.

They show even more thoroughly in their showing,

and in showing more thoroughly they illuminate and safeguard more thoroughly in the turning overcoming.

The signs of the inceptual beginning of the inception.

The signs and the footpaths: the showing, the signs, the greetings, the hints.

The task is to think the essence of showing in terms of the overcoming, which has been thought in a more originally alethetic manner.

Bringing the sign closer and carrying it away.

Fulfilling in showing in the midst of the clearing and in forging into concealment.

33. σῆμα – θῆμα

positing – placing – *setting up* – letting appear
something which itself indicates something,
the *tribute*, which calls attention to ...
attribute
letting appear
unconcealing concealing and sheltering

34. Word and Sign

The word is not a sign, or at least it is not a sign in terms of the sign considered from the outside or considered in terms of sound.

If it is thought in an originary manner, then the sign is preserved in the essence of the word.

The word – the soundless illuminating voice of beyng.

The claim – the showing that shows itself in overcoming.

The simple element of the sign is not the formal element of the sign as a material thing.

35. The Sign

The customary consideration of the "symbolic" in terms of "meaning" can be formulated as:

something means something, i.e. something shows itself *as* something.

What to make of the "as?" Where does it come from? What is this "something as something" grounded in?

Differentiation – beings *as* beings! Beings *and* being.

The potential to formalize the relation "something as something" into a "sign" – "symbol": everything is and is everywhere and constantly a "sign" *of* something "*for*" something ("*representing*"). Formalization as the shadowing aspect of the corrupted essence, which accompanies all thinking of being.

Hence also the talk of: "being of beings" is an empty phrase and for most people it remains *only* that.

The modern world is full of ciphers and symbols and is nonetheless without a sign.

36. The Sign and Safeguarding – The Departing Abyssal Ground

Concealment originates from the safeguarding essence of truth.

The essential prevailing of showing takes its essential prevailing from the safeguarding which conceals.

37. The Sign Bound to the Event

Showing enables the encountering of illuminated being by guiding the way there.

Showing is the form of "bequeathing" appropriate to beings as they are in the event and this bequeathing leads to the safeguarding and vigilance for the inception.

When are signs illuminated? Only when the claim of beyng appropriates itself and offers a hint into the truth of beyng.

Beings then become something that shows; yet they do not show themselves as objects and do not show the way into the progression of objects, rather they lead the way into beyng, for beings themselves are extracted from beinglessness beforehand and are drawn out of the clearing of beyng. There are signs only when the event essences. Showing arises from beings appropriated in the inception. The showing of the sign is not a form of indication set into motion by representation. The showing of the sign is the happening of the event itself.

The sign and differentiation.

The essence of the sign in the mode of departure.

38. Event – Aptitude – Sign

Sign – it is illuminated bequeathing indication (showing) leading into the departure of the overcoming of being. The sign is the abyss of the inceptual beginning *bound to the event*. (What does it indicate? Safeguarding and preservation and the truth of beyng.)

Even in the broader conception of the sign, it is still only comprehended metaphysically in an objective-technical fashion. So too is the "symbol" comprehended in this way – and that is where the "sign" as thing, the sign as structure and what is signified all *collapse together*.

The sign bound to the event never "signifies," for the showing of inceptual signs "presents" nothing and "represents" nothing; even less so is the sign bound to the event a cipher, for ciphers only exist where the differentiation between the rational and irrational dominates the essence of truth with undiminished force.

The sign shows the way into the abyssal ground, it elevates into overcoming, and is of the manner of bequeathing *appropriation*. As bequeathing appropriation, the event accrues essentially to the human being. Which ones are the *signs*? Every being is a sign. It is a sign as soon as it is aptly illuminated within being, and aptly illuminated within the showing into the event.

The most inconspicuous element lacking any intrusive force of its own – that is a sign.

39. Truth as Error – The Signlessness of Error

Errancy [Irre] as the establishment of the securing of order.
Errancy and mad-ness [*Irr-sinn*]

The mad [*Irrsinnigen*] and the comet [*Irrstern*].
The comet and earth.
Earth and the truth.

40. The Sign

The sign essences out of the decisive counter-turning force of the event.
It essences in the mode of departure.

That is because the human must already or must explicitly be *appropriated* for the inception, if he is to be open for the signs. The human is not an obtuse thing, who is then steered toward a sign – if that were the case, then the sign would remain *inaccessible.*

Word and comprehension.
The inceptual word – that which shows, appropriating all that shows.
Sound and sign.
Sign and meaning.
The universal *metaphysical* dominance of the sign in the first inception.
σήματα σημαίνει
Sign and differentiation.

41. The Essence of the Sign in the Mode of Departure

The characteristic trait: the metaphysical *signum* –
depicting *in terms of presence* and directing into beings.
The sign – as *intimation* directing into the abyssal ground.
The inceptual essence of the sign can only be experienced within the *turn* itself, i.e. within the domain of the truth of beyng.

The sign and the turn.
The turn – *the inceptual sign itself.*
Sign – it does not refer to the human, rather the sign is essential prevailing of beyng and only once it has become the essence prevailing can it be *as* the essential in reference to the human.

*

Being as presence – (the fundamental trait of beingness and all metaphysical determination and precisely where being is regarded as becoming)
Being as departure – (the fundamental trait of the inceptual essence of beyng)

Presence directed toward beings and their predominance – domination and actuality, order.

Departure – away from beings, i.e. away from their presumption of priority, and yet this departure is not a disengagement, rather it is a way of *cutting off* through departure [*Ab*schied]; – it is not mere presence, rather it is the failure of overcoming leading into the downfall as the inceptual beginning of the abyssal ground.

Departure – the incalculable *persistence*, which is only experienced in the anguish of separation.

Those who are most divided: those who are most proximal.

*

Any attempt to turn the inceptuality of language into a technology of everyday speech runs counter to the essence of language.

The inceptuality of language in itself already demands the execution of the leap into the inceptual beginning and this inceptuality does not tolerate any negotiation or mediation. Negotiation and mediation [can] impart nothing to transformation.

42. Sign and Greeting

Showing into that which is greeting.
The greeting of beyng – inception.
The greeting of the holy.

43. Word and Sign

Are words signs?
Are vocabulary words signs?
What is a sign?
How do we perceive the word?
We do not possess the essential origin outright, nor do we possess the word or the sign outright.

44. The Objective Essence of the Sign

– that is of a metaphysical origin.
Sensible – Nonsensible.

Sensible – senseless above nonsensible.

The objective element arising from *presencing* (glancing in the direction of something).

σῆμα – τέχνη.

The mere act of setting the event-bound origin of the sign in relief against its objective essence narrows the gaze and also sets the gaze askance; this contrast is nothing more than a stopgap measure in aid of the first communication.

*

Symbols, symptoms, characters, traits,

Signs of characteristics, marks [*Kennzeichen, Merkzeichen*].

45. "Sign"
(Sign as Tool in *Being and Time*)[29]

Signs in the mode of things show in a different manner and upon a different ground from vocal expression, gestures or hand signals. These can all be regarded as living signs, the kind of signs which appear within the purview of a particular life form [*Lebewesens*]: its "movements" express something for us. Regarded in the broadest sense, the declarations announced by these movements aim at something internal, which then comes out through the declaration. Even just in this description, "inside" and "outside" already count as the fundamental scheme of living things.

Anything that expresses the internal in this way signifies the internal. Whether the expression could show something else and show how it might be able to do so, or whether it might be able to show something distinct, revealing something specific about the life form which expresses *itself* in this way, and whether this showing might even be regarded as an offering or even an opening up of beings as such – none of this could be decided by observing the mere form of expression employed by this being.

One thing alone becomes immediately clear, namely that "expression" is not sufficient to comprehend the showing of the word and language. Instead, expression is transferred over to something else, for example to works of art.

---

[29] Martin Heidegger, *Being and Time: A Translation of* Sein und Zeit, trans. Joan Stambaugh, ed. Dennis Schmidt (Albany, NY: SUNY Press, 2010), § 17.

"Signs" as *things* and as *modes of expression*, but also signs as *language* in the narrower sense, they all arise within beings as beings (objects in the broadest sense). The sign *bound to the event* as the essential inception of all showing cannot at all be compared to the sign as a mode of expression.

46. The Sign as Thing

The sign is a thing in terms of equipment. It is not only a thing as something that shows, but it is also a thing in its "showing" and in what is shown, while, for example, the direction and indication of an arrow or the marking of a paving stone only "refer to" relations within beings and are themselves something which is present. The signpost stands at the crossroads – the hands of the clock glide over the digits.

Is what is shown always and necessarily also a being? Indeed – even where the metaphysical sign is referred to and the empirical dimension is turned into a symbol of the supersensible, the supersensible is meant [?][30] as a being. This is the case even where the sign is measured against the kind of object which is known as a "natural thing," or is even referred to as something "immaterial." The "transcendent" ("transcendence") is a being ("being" in terms of the usual confused chatter).

Moreover, the sign here is thought from the perspective of that which shows itself (sensible thing), just as it is thought everywhere else. Showing – showing the way from this to something Other. Even if it is thought in terms of the event [*ereignishaft*], the Other is not only beyng and the truth of beyng, rather it is what shows itself.

47. Showing and Symbol

What is essential to the "symbol" in the literal understanding of the terms is that is a concordance of something as the selfsame. This essential configuration of concordance grounds and endows a specific multiplicity of signs. Yet this configuration itself not does not exclusively refer to the creation of signs, nor is it limited to the creation of signs. Insofar as every sign in the form of a thing is based on at least one

---

[30] {TN: included in the original.}

agreed-upon appointment in the broadest sense of the term, then all of these signs are "symbols" in the strict sense of the term. Admittedly, then, the word "symbol" would acquire a dominant meaning, which would purportedly "depict" the peculiar unity of that which shows and what is shown. Here metaphysics and mysticism, the degenerate form of metaphysics, begin to assert their particular mode of opining.

Are there "natural" signs? Natural signs refer to the sort of things which have naturally grown within beings. These signs are natural to the extent that their emergence is the result of a natural process of growth. Likewise, what they signify and the manner in which they follow the sign and how they make use of it are the result of a natural process of growth – bird calls or atmospheric conditions guiding lifeforms. But are these nothing more than immediate causal nexuses, which we merely interpret in a symbolic manner?

48. The Objective Miscalculation of Signs and Symbols

One might ask to what extent the sign coincides with what it signifies, and from which perspectives and under which circumstances it might do so. Let us say one has two objects before him, the symbol and the symbolized, and then he calculates out whether and how the particular attribute in the symbol reappears in an identical (or similar?) manner in what is symbolized. After all, something or other that is identical must be found amid all the dissimilarity between the two. Resemblance and coinciding are based upon this identity – what is completely disparate could of course never be reduced to a *sym-bolon*.

49. On the Sign in § 17f. of *Being and Time*

Only the sign as tool is thought in that passage; at the same time, however, the passage stresses how, in each thing signified by a sign, the world-character appears (total relevance, cf. p. 82f.).[31]

The passage regards the sign ontically and elucidates the sign's character as equipment. The passage interprets showing as a form of reference. The elucidation of the essence of the sign is only carried out in the service of a broader demarcation of the concept of the world. But now both showing and the sign not only can be, but indeed must be – and

---

[31] Heidegger, *Being and Time*, 82.

specifically based upon the experience of the originary essence of the truth of beyng – thought in a simpler and simultaneously more steadfast manner. If such thinking were carried out, however, then what is said in § 17 and § 18 would no longer be expounded upon in a direct way, as if the foundations for the experience of the essence of the sign were laid there. Rather, the truth of beyng, the inceptual essence of the sign is illuminated based on the acquired knowledge of what the path in that passage seeks to achieve. Consequently, the sign as thing and sign as equipment of showing can be thought in a more suitable manner in these terms. It would be a gross misinterpretation if one were to think that the aforementioned paragraphs contain *the* sole statement about the essence of the sign.

50. Showing and Reference

Reference means more than the mere re-presentation and letting-beseen of something. Reference involves interaction and the path and the *sojourn* (being-in-the-world). Reference is not the mere task of taking note. Yet *reference* now regarded in terms of the ready-to-hand as *usefulness for* ...; this, for example, already contains instructions for possible use and interaction and, in that way, it opens up what essences in such a reference. The referential totality is relevance.

51. The Sign as the "As"

Re-presenting something as something –
something depicts itself as something,
shows itself and indeed it does so *in each case* "as ..."

If we regard it from the standpoint of the "subject" of the human, the "as" is a projecting incursion and a preconception.

If experienced in a manner bound to the event, the "as" is the happening of the event of the clearing – and within it what happens as event is suitable to the truth.

52. The Sign and the Attribute

Noticing of the attention of attending.
The *moment* [Mal].
Sign – symbol – image.

53. The Sign

What priority does the sign as thing have? The sign and metaphysics: the sign appears to reside in the distinction between and the indication of the sensible and non-sensible. It would, however, be a misrecognition of the alethic-event-bound essence of showing to believe this. This misrecognition is reinforced in the sensible-intuitive character of the sign as thing as it appears in its initial interpretation. Metaphysics impedes the inceptual consternation caused by signs. Metaphysics enables and fosters the invention of the symbolic.

54. Sign and Signal

Not every sign is a signal, yet, by contrast, every signal is a sign. Not every signal is an alarm signal in the sense of a signal that issues a call to arms, gathers together in readiness for something, or merely awakens us to it. Then again, a warning signal is unlike such signals and so too is a "signal" which merely calls attention to something. A signal which indicates, for example, the proximity of a curve or an entry ramp is also of a different kind. The sign which merely indicates restricts itself to the letting appear of something present, which might include something which one is approaching toward or something which is arriving. The indicating sign nevertheless may never be regarded as the fundamental form of the sign, while the other forms of signs are interpreted in terms of that fundamental form. The fundamental form is determined by the alethic essence of the sign. The fundamental trait of the essence of the sign is concealing sheltering. This concealing sheltering above all determines each instance of illumination, and only then does it determine in a uniform manner the ways in which the sign shows itself.
1.   The inceptually self-showing sign (bound to the event).
2.   Signs set up and installed (signals).
3.   The appointed "sign" of concordance.
4.   The sign of inceptual origin essencing in the word.

III. THE WORD. CONVERSATION AND LANGUAGE

55. Hint

The word appropriates the human.
(That is a saying of coming history; not a timeless essential proposition.)
The appropriated human is he who stands within the expropriation of the event.
Steadfastness is the layered past of shepherded en-couragement.
Who is the human? The *appropriated one* of the word.
The event words [*wortet*].
Prior to that: The human is ζῷον (animal) λόγον ἔχον, the indeterminate element of λόγος.

56. Thanking

– appropriated guiding into the hints of the truth of beyng –
freeing and bringing.

57. Thanking as Appropriated Guiding into the Hints

Letting oneself be terrified by the quiet benevolence cast over the gentle ushering.
That is an occasion for attentiveness to the concealed hint of the inception.
Often it is something barely noticeable, grazing us as it passes by. Out of this inconspicuousness astonishment awakens over a stillness hitherto unsuspected, a stillness which quietly lets everything rest within itself.
Thanks
Thought
Thinking, thanking (Cf. hints)[32]

58. Thinking

We think –
We are safeguarded beneath the *unthinkable* and we wander (Hölderlin) into what cannot be thought in advance.

[32] Planned for inclusion in Volume 101.

Thus safeguarding is.

We *think* – we experience the round dance of our surroundings, which is the *homeland*.

The more rigorously we think, the more gently the unthinkable indulges in preparation through thinking.

Thinking and thanking.

*

Steadfastness
– dwelling within the round dance occurs in steadfastness;
the *unthinkable*.

59. Language and Word

Language arising from their opposition – and thus the semblance of equivalence – and thus immediately misinterpreted.

1. ἄνθρωπος ζῷον λόγον ἔχον
   Language – what the human has – *essential possession*
   The *human* as animal (inceptually φύσις – ζωή the upsurging, whose upsurge is conjoined through gathering, presencing, discourse, saga, language).
2. The word which the human (Da-sein) "has" (essential prevailing of the word), grounding – abyssal [*ab-gründig*].

Here everything is different and not simply as a condition, nor as a different opinion and theory; it is not as the reversal of fixed variables (human – language), rather the *transition* into the *transformation* of the reference to beyng and steadfastness in its truth.

Constancy of stillness – the essential prevailing of the word as attuning "voice."

The transition – taking it over historically, understanding the hints – the reference to beyng as the encouragement of beyng.

Thinking as transitional (beyng-historical)

Thinking up (moving away, projecting!) –

but projection as beyng itself – not as beings.

60. Indication and Pointing

Pointing out [An-deuten]
sheltering ανα- beginning tomorrow

closer – upwards – *forth and back*
pointing *bound to the event*
Unconcealing-concealing sheltering
expropriating
Pointing [Andeutung], not meaning [*Bedeutung*] is the *treasure of the word.*
saying and contradiction, perceiving – giving.

61. The Authentic Conversation

Bringing – freeing
Yet in freeing being appropriated into *what brings* and *what is brought*, bequeathed into bringing into freeing.
the counter-echo as harmony directing into the appropriating movement.

62. The Reification of Language

The reification of language in the manner conceived by metaphysics is commonly thought to be in verbal articulation (rendering sensible).

But reification, if reification can at all be thought, is the beings of language, it is the layered past of language, is the conversation as what is appropriated.

63. Language and Poetry

It is not enough if, instead of dissecting common language grammatically, and instead of explaining it and representing it in the universal, we now select poetic language as the target for the same accusation in order to carry out the same procedure on it.

Poetry itself is indeed the concealed element of the word and can only be thought in terms of this concealed element and, consequently, in terms of the event.

The reference to poesy and to the idea that language in its primordial mode is "poetry" only seemingly says the authentic.

Even if we were to think in this way, we would still stand outside of the ring of the event.

64. All Thinking about Language Hitherto

All thinking about language hitherto is *metaphysics* and remains caught between φωνή and νοήματα. And then there is the corresponding array of disciplines.

"Language" as "object" of philosophical analysis.

But the metaphysical analysis of language creeps in everywhere. The overcoming of metaphysics becomes most arduous and difficult where that occurs.

Here, however, even the definitive element of the transition is most proximal.

The task is to think the essence of beyng in terms of the word and to think the human as appropriated in the word – the word as the departure into the ring.

Becoming attentive to beyng, that means being circumspect for the truth of beyng.

*

The *word* is the tolling light of the event.

65. The Authentic Conversation

pointing, silently waiting,
preserving-revering
unprecedented saying of assent [*Zu-sagen*] to another – and re-peating
to oneself [*Sich-Über-sagen*].[33]
Bringing – *freeing* – echoing back as harmony leading into unification.
Perceiving – what speaks in the conversation bestows upon all sides.
Saying is listening and listening is saying.
The allusion in the authentic conversation.

*

Conversation is the homeland of language.

*

[33] {TN: The outdated verb *übersagen* most commonly means "to convict," specifically by means of witness testimony. Given the use of the reflexive pronoun "sich," I have chosen the less common meaning of repeating to oneself, especially in order to learn something by heart.}

Conversation and the mother tongue,
mother tongue and language.
"language" –   1. *the speaking language* – the Speaking[34] word
                 2. the *spoken language* and the one that can be found in
                    its linguistic content.

66. Logic

From the origin of the word through the future (historical) link
between thinking and poetry.
The *thought of thanks*,
the beyng-historical determination of thinking.

67. Language and φύσις

Language is each respective sending of the word. Language is
historical – never "natural" in the sense of an urge compelled by nature.
    φύσις can never be thought in terms of the *physical* and the natural.
Φύσις – ascent,

shelters $\left\{\begin{array}{l}\text{flourishing resting within itself (nature)}\\\text{and}\\\text{sending and "layered past"}\end{array}\right.$

68. Becoming Attentive to Beyng (Event)

Becoming attentive to beyng through
circumspection for the preserving truth of beyng.
Circumspection originates from guarding.
Shepherds let guarding be experienced (teaching in wandering).

69. Word – Truth of Language

That which is immemorial, terrifying, surpassing,
compelling in the word.

[34] {TN: capitalized in the original.}

70. Out of the Rare Moments

The task is to contemplate language from these rare moments of *authentic* conversation.

The authentic conversation is the *happening as event leading into the word* driven by the inclination of the mantra (neither mere gawking, nor active life – everything based on beings).
The authentic conversation and the truth of beyng.
Words – authentic, i.e. belonging into the event – appropriated out of the event.

71. Language and the Conversation

The conversation – in the authentic sense – speaks from the mantra of beyng, whose word is the tolling light of the event.
Language is the happening of the event – historical.
Insofar as it can be willed, produced, performed.
About what, how, with whom, and why is there speaking.
The merely *material conversation – "abstract."*

*

Conversation and monologue.

72. "Meaning"

Meant here in terms of "meaningful," "weighty," a matter of importance – *a meaningful achievement – something which prompts one to think.*

73. The Preserving Truth of Language

This is never thought in terms of correctness and never thought in reference to vocabulary or starting from vocabulary;
   therefore 1. preserving truth (expropriation)
           2. *the* word (*the* vocabulary) – "*the words*"
            the mantra.

74. Beyng and Aspect

Saying and word
Beyng as *event*
Property
Being given away.

75. Signification of Meaning

Indicate in the direction of – by – ἀμφί
Giving to understand
by pointing – conferring.
pointing – *hinting* – event.
The *word* – stillness – the preserving truth of beyng.
The truth – of language.
Not the "vocabulary" that has meaning and *not* language.
But the *sound* and the *staff* [Stab] (sign), *book* staff [Buch-*stab*],[35] *litera*.
Sounding.
Play.
Circumspection and *guarding*.
Through the guarding of the *shepherds* the *circumspectness* arises for others to adopt.
and so too does the hesitation.

76. Word and Language

Language is the *preserving* of truth [Wahr-*heit*] appropriated in encouragement from the word,
it is the *event* native within [*ein-heimsche*] beyngs [*Seyenden*].

77. "Logic"

Outside of the sole task required for this reflection, there are other endeavors.

---

[35] Heidegger is playing with the component words of *Buchstabe*, which means "letter" in the sense of the letters of the alphabet. *Buch* means book, while *Stabe* is a derivative of *Stab* (staff).

There is something concerned with knowledge about the essence of language, it perhaps might even enable the improvement of linguistics and philosophy.
But it provides no hints in that direction – *only other trails*;
Clearly and simply it leads to these other trails, but they are long and arduous.

*

Yet being appropriates itself out of the nothing.
Thus it is from the happening of the event.
The sparks [?][36] *of the illuminating light*, which, on rare occasions, enable beings and the nothingless to first come to their own property, only to then let them escape it again.
Beyng does not always essence.
That which is *nothingless* does not even permit it – the *nothing* – to name [that] which is not.
There *is not even nothing* in nothinglessness.

78. How the Saying of Language

How is the saying of language in conversation a bringing and freeing?
How do bringing and freeing have their silence and intimacy in the bounty of the homeland?

79. That We are Speechless

– to what extent are we speechless?
bereft of silence [*schweiglos*]: –
bereft of the event [*ereignislos*]

80. The Word – The Human

The word (the stillness of appropriation) appropriates the human of steadfastness within the preserving truth of beyng.

---

[36] {TN: included in the original.}

81. Language and Correspondence

The correspondence of the prelude and preliminary thinking,
with language first arising from it.
Yet the correspondence is appropriated. This occurs because
preparatory thinking and the prelude are each impoverished in their
own way.

82. Articulation and Listening

Listening as appropriated per-ception – acquisition into steadfastness.

Sound – this is not thought from the perspective of writing as a
material symbol which serves as a placeholder and takes the place of
meaning.

Sounding out – letting something toll – corresponding reception,
happening as event [*er-eignen*] leading into affinity to being. This does
not reach the point of objectification or the point of reckoning, with
the symbols standing in for vocabulary words [*Wörterzeichen*].

The *"fleetingness" of sound corresponds to the originary beginning of
the moment.*

Tolling and bringing – initial sounding.

The word leads us up to something – yet does *not* deliver it over.

What part of us is involved and how do the words bring it to us? And
upon what occasion?

83. Language

The 6 pages of § 34 in *Being and Time* about Da-sein, discourse, and
language *are among the most essential* – and they have, despite the
fact that they have been silenced everywhere, "had an impact," even
though they have not actually been contemplated in a more originary
manner.[37]

Everything is still clumsy and ensnared in the confusion of the dis-
entanglement and caught up in the separation from metaphysics and
yet – if we attend to what is simple.

---

[37] Heidegger, *Being and Time*, 155–161.

84. How There is Within "Language"

How is there within "language" intimating, guiding, compelling, surpassing, startling, something unthinkable in advance (word – beyng), halting and delaying, ascending?

The conversation that speaks the mantra of beyng is the *sounding light of the event.*

Conversation – is not a product and not an achievement, rather it is *appropriated.*

85. We are Speech-less

The exhaustion of our language.
The festival, the fixity of the word[38]
  and
the lack of restraint involved in discourse.

The frenzy of achievement –
The inability to listen.

86. Animal and Language

"For the mute animal, the world is One impression, and for lack of the number two, it does not even count as one." (Hofmannsthal)[39]
"the world?" – "impression"
One impression – how is that to be understood?
For it is precisely not a world, it is not the scission of world and earth from the event.

87. Grammar – Logic – Language

Jean Paul:
"But grammar – as the logic of the tongue, as the first philosophy of reflection – decides; for it elevates the signs of things themselves back

---

[38] Heidegger writes "*das Fest[e]*" and thus achieves a double meaning of the festival (*das Fest*) and that which is fixed or firm (*das Feste*).

[39] Hugo von Hoffmansthal, *Wert und Ehre Deutscher Sprache: In Zeugnissen* (Munich: Verlag der Bremer Presse, 1927).

to things and forces the mind [*Geist*], now turned back toward itself, to observe its own operation of observation, i.e. it forces the mind to reflect; it forces the mind to at least regard the (language-)sign as more solid, and not to conflate it, as if it were a proclamation, with sensation itself." (Hofmannsthal, 126)[40]

"Every good grammarian is part philosopher and only a philosopher would write the best grammar." (Hoffmansthal, 127)[41]

88. Saying and Forming Images

Word and image
The word searches for the image.
The image searches for the word – G[oethe][42]
The search for both
Word and tone.
Images do not provide the truth.
They only illuminate, for as viewpoints they bear luminescence in themselves and thus can illuminate in manifold ways.

89. The Native and the Foreign Element

The native and the foreign element
of discourse and of vocabulary –
always underway, climbing and falling,
expanse and narrowness.

[40] Ibid., 126.
[41] Ibid., 127.
[42] Ibid., 117: "Word and image are correlates which continually search for one another ..."

90. [Event and Language]

91. Language and Thinking

Language – the quietest and most loyal confidant of thinking, expropriated from the unity of property.

92. Conversation – the Metamorphosis of Encouragement

Conversation is not only the expression and articulation of disparate relations, rather, as the metamorphosis of the attribution, conversation is in itself the quietest reference produced by humans and issued *to* one another (not merely with one another). They issue this reference to one another along the ways of the footpaths.

Conversation – is not continuous discourse; silence, being surprised, the unexpected, the inexpressible – yet precisely in *saying* – the *remaining*.

93. The Unnecessary and Language

Language as the concealed counselor of peoples [*Ratgeberin der Völker*].[43]

But this does not mean to regard language as an arbitrary inventory of words, but instead to regard the word imbedded in the jewelry of the stillest glimmer of the conjoined word. The most distant disposition and most intimate thinking are conserved in that conjuncture.

---

[43] {TN: Counselor [*Ratgeberin*] is gendered feminine.}

94. Conversation and Encouragement

Harmonious sound
sweetness
clumsy attempts
the hesitating
sudden ringing out

95. Conversation and διαλέγεσθαι

There is already metaphysics here.
ἰδέα – παιδεία – κοινόν

96. Language and Preserving Truth

Language as saga preserves the event, it preserves the in-expressible and preserves what cannot be thought in advance; it preserves what has been and what will come. Where language speaks (talks) of what is present, it often produces chatter and drivel.

Language both preserves *and* squanders, it exploits and distorts, it lays waste to the *safeguarding element of the truth of beyng.*

Language preserves the event – for language emerges from the word and remains with the word. Language is the *promise* of the event granted to the appropriated human. In language and as language, the word of beyng promises truth (the spoken promise).

Speaking and *promising.*

97. The Word Comes to Language, Beyng Brings itself to the Word

The *word* is a *bringing* of a unique kind.

In happening as event, the word brings the very thing we have not yet conjectured under *suspicion* [Vermuten], and this suspicion is already presaged [*angemutet*].

98. Pro-mising

Not the usual and self-evident form of promising, rather the one that was not conjectured – the sole one – this is something entirely unusual and something incapable of being fixed in the form of an accomplishment.

The promise (authentic) is mysterious. The promise conserves the fulfillment, saves it.

The conserving element in the promise.

Pro-mise as be-ginning.

Be-ginning and de-cision.

Decision – execution.

"fulfillment" – not subsequently affixed, rather in the promise.

Be-gins the ful-fillment.

The coming and the transformation.

Promises and *auguring* (to be called – bearing the *name*),

letting the *name be carried* and *letting it belong to beyng.*

99. Pro-mising and Receiving and Keeping the Word

Promising – making visible? No; declaration of one's intentions? No. But it is *saying assent* [zu-sagen] to what comes as what remains.

Pro-mising – letting come and *preserving* this, the preserving of coming, sending and preserving – guaranteeing.

Can a person ever promise something? It is most likely to happen where the person himself has already been suitably appropriated.

To *keep* the "word" and to *break* the "word" ..., give one's *word* thereupon, the *promise given.*

In language, in its vocabulary, and in its saying, the *word is given* to the human, while beyng is *promised over* [ver-sprochen] to him.

The *promise is kept* – but to what extent and why? The question is whether and how the human *receives and accepts the promise, sticks to the promise*, i.e. the question is the extent to which he remains steadfast.

Promising bound to the event – the *requisitioning appropriation* of the word into language, *relinquishing the word into language.* According to this, it is also language alone which is pro-mised, but for the most part this happens unnoticed.

100. Conversation (Authentic)

Conversation is *not* communication – declaration – instructing. There is no schema for the essential definition of the conversation other than the word itself.

But word as the word of beyng and beyng ⟺ human.

"Conversation" – in contrast to acting and accomplishment – seems to be mere talk and chatter; it seems as if nothing takes place in the conversation, and yet everything takes place there. All doing and letting is a result or bearing out of the conversation.

Conversation – steadfastness in the word; hesitating, surpassing, timidity, audacity, the unsuspected and suspicion.

101. Moment and Conversation

We are each in conversation in the *moment of vision* [Augen-blick] and speak out of the *moment of vision*.

The eye *casts a glance* and *renders visible*. Perhaps rendering visible is more originary, so that all beholding is within it.

Eyesight.

We are *not only thinking* about glancing as *capturing, receiving*, as *doing*. Why?

ῥοπή ὀφθαλμοῦ ῥέπω – to incline – scrunching up the eyebrows – blocking someone's view, the preponderance to one side – *deflection point discrimen momentum* – decision, surge, jolt, *what tips the scales*. We understand the *moment* from the perspective of *momentum* and ῥοπή. How does the *moment* come to *momentum* – *surge*, jolt – but whose? Yet not only the *processual*, rather the *glance of the eye* serve as the deflection point – they are decisive.

In the blink of an eye? The *sudden moment*? Something that is without a before and after, rather it has only a *whither* [wo-her]? This is regarded everywhere in terms of the passing of time.

102. The Moment

There are moments when beyng tolls purely from itself as the play of freedom of the inception and then it fades away into its own stillness. Tolling appropriates the clearing more than anything else. It is this clearing into which its own shining peers in. There it first gains a form of vision which can glimpse the illuminating shelter.

The momentous element of the moment is not the fleeing instant in which something passes by, rather the momentous is what cannot be produced or explained, but it is also the inephemeral element of the glancing act of active imagining of attendant seeing.

103. The Word and the Veil

σημαίνειν – unconcealing – concealing
showing – as guiding into truth
giving to understand

104. Language – Speaking – Discourse

Conversation – mantra (the conversation speaks the attribution) spoken from it.
Saga – failure to say.
Conversation and promise.

IV. THE WORD

(Footpaths of the Inception)
Event
(CF. POETIZING AND THINKING)
(Steadfastness)

105. The Word-Play

Customarily understood as: playing with words and their meaning.
How is that possible?
Word and play –
Does the world itself arise from the play of graceful thinking?

106. The Word

Language – word – voice – stillness – happening of the event
tone – play – letting – inquiring – freedom
"sound"

107. The Word – The Meaning of Vocabulary[44]

As soon as we begin to speak about the "meaning" of "words," we have connected them to their wording [*Wortlaut*], and that wording has a

---

[44] First published in Dietrich Papenfuss and Otto Pöggeler, eds., *Im Spiegel der Welt: Sprache, Übersetzung, Auseinandersetzung (Zur philosophischen Aktualität Heideggers*, vol. 3) (Frankfurt am Main: Vittorio Klostermann, 1992), 13–16.

"meaning" affixed to it. As a sensible given, sound (φωνή) is the most proximal and actual. Everything else is attached to it and thrust upon it so that the word becomes the bearer of meaning as the structure of sounds.

Can this easily be proven and confirmed at any moment based on the factual situation of language? Certainly it can be. But is it enough to say that language is thereby thought of in terms of its "inception?" If we take stock of language based on wording [*Wortlaut*], then meaning arises within the essential question: what is language? Of what is language comprised? One can easily recognize the metaphysical character of such stock-taking. The sonorous and sounding out have physical properties. Meaning in turn is what is not sensible (sense), i.e. the metaphysical. Yet if we consider the matter more precisely, the factual situation actually reveals itself to be quite different. The sounding word and the object signified by the word are given (the thing, for example). Only by assuming that the word "signifies" the thing, while in contrast the sound itself merely sounds and rings out, one could arrive at the function of the word in signification with the help of what can neither be the mere sounding of the word, nor the thing signified: but that is the "meaning."

This gives rise to the further question of how this whole apparatus is to be classified. One commonly relinquishes it to representation and opining. In doing so, one has unwittingly stumbled into the terrain which determines the relation of the human to beings. This occurs insofar as the coincidence between representation and object is possible in this terrain. This coincidence is called "truth." The aforementioned stock-taking of the essence of the word and language not only presupposes knowledge of beings and presupposes knowledge of the human, but it likewise moves within the space of an essence of truth which has been unwittingly adopted. From that point on, all elucidation of language and the word moves within the terrain thus constituted, which is obviously the terrain of metaphysics. Metaphysics furnishes the components of the philosophy of language and furnishes the components of linguistic research, yet it also furnishes, immediately and unwittingly, the surrounding field of potential viewpoints between which the diverse theories course back and forth.

Yet if metaphysics as such is not inceptual, then all previous "knowledge" of language fails to be true knowledge.

Yet why should such inceptual knowledge at all be necessary? It is certainly not because this knowledge is dependent upon an orderly institution of research. Rather, it is necessary because the word, along with the manner in which the word is, both play a part in deciding the destiny of the human.

If we take contemplation "about" the word as our goal, then any attempt to refurbish linguistics would simply prove to be a highly impoverished terrain of movement for thinking. Yet neither the threat to the human posed by the downfall of language, nor the threat posed by the debasement of the word are sufficient to justify the thinking "about" the word, a thinking which bears the semblance of reflection. Moreover, the downfall of language is perhaps merely a consequence of the threat to the human being, and it is this threat which forms a different source. It arises from the forgetting of being.

Yet the word could even belong to the truth of beyng. If that were the case, then it would only be appropriate to say the word in terms of the inceptual thinking of beyng. Then, in turn, it would be necessary to clarify, in terms of the inceptual thinking of beyng, what relevance that thinking has to meaning in relation to the remaining components of language, specifically with regard to what one calls "the soul," designating it in contrast to the embodied word [*Wortleib*]. If metaphysics does in fact get something right, then the aspect of what it gets right must still be thought in its origin, without regard for the status of its truth.

It is not for the sake of the human being that inceptual thinking contemplates the word; rather, inceptual thinking contemplates the word of gratitude to beyng.

Thus it could happen [*sich ereignen*] that the well-known components of language reveal themselves to be of a different "kind." A simple consideration could lead into the free space of thinking.

Customarily, words in terms of vocabulary refer to the structured context of speaking in the conversation of language, that is to say, they refer to beings. Every "something" which is uttered in a conversation is a being.

However, yet another spoken element which is not reducible to an utterance remains concealed in conversation. Precisely this word just named – "is" – says "something" which a "being" is not; the word names beyng.

Is it, this word, its variations and the concealed forms in the structure of language, only an exception among the words of a vocabulary, is this word an outsider harbored within the linguistic stock, or is it the word of all words? Is it the word within which all other words of a vocabulary first come to be words? If that were so, then we might be obligated to conclude that, whether the process is articulated or not, beyng first bestows on beings their appearance and their self-showing in such a way that beings become the sort of thing which can be signified. In other words, it is only through this bestowal that beings can be that which is signified and can be signification in the commonly understood meaning of those terms.

If that were the case, then beyng would first grant to beings this: that beings, in their appearing and self-illumination, indicate an Other. Beyng, then, would first endow beings with the very possibility of having a meaning. Beyng, then, is that which endows beings with such meanings and grants them significant meaning [*be-deutet*]. Beyng (as the inceptual thanks) instills these [*be-denkt*] beings with these meanings through thinking. Beyng is that which signifies meaning [*das Be-deutende*].

Thus, in contrast to the metaphysics of language, something else arises from this in the form of an Other: it is not that the sound of the word means and signifies an object with the aid of a "meaning" which attaches to it from somewhere or other, rather it is the case that beyng bears significant meaning [*be-deutet*] (in a manner bound to the event) and displaces it to beings as such. This occurs in such a way that beyng happens as event in the pointing and showing of the inceptual signs. And what happens as event is, consequently, the word in its initial form and initially is only comprehended according to its mere sound, and then that sound is subsequently furnished with "meaning."

The conversation overlooks what is said authentically in language to the extent that the conversation represents and grasps only what is uttered.

It should not at all come as a surprise that "is" and "being" are only permitted as helping words [*Hilfs-wörter*].

It is only because language arises from the saga of beyng that it can become language. But the saga of beyng can never be thought or experienced in terms of language, nor in terms of the metaphysical explication of language.

Nonetheless, in an inceptual sense, the word "being" is the helping word plain and simple to the extent that it first helps deliver language to itself, and it does so even where this inconspicuous word stays behind and remains in the unconcealment of that which is inceptual.

With this word (being, is ...), the human has already received the guarantee that, prior to all beings, beyng is said and sayable. But, at the same time, that creates the danger of only explaining the word from the standpoint of language and thus it creates the danger of blocking thinking from the path which contemplates the inception of language.

The human has language because language arises in the word, yet the word has the human as the saga of beyng, that is to say, that the word determines the human in his calling [*Bestimmung*]. The voice of beyng is that which determines and attunes [*Be-stimmende*]. This voice does not ring out; rather, it keeps itself silent in the stillness created by twisting free from beyng and moves toward the truth of the overcoming of being (silencing and veiling).

Should it ever prove necessary to contemplate thinking and poetry in their inceptual origin and in their inceptual destiny, then this could only be possible from the knowledge of the word and its inceptual beginning and destiny. The resulting contemplation would express gratitude to beyng. Such a necessity would not be motivated by poesy or philosophy itself, much less by that late institutional form of these activities known as culture. The appeal to and regard for language, much like the appeal to and regard for the "word" understood in terms of language – those are all errant paths.

Yet if beyng in its truth is the overcoming leading into the departure, and if the arrival of the sheltering of the inception bestows itself within the departure, and if beyng is the event of appropriation (namely as the turn from scission and arrival), is favor and gratitude, then under these conditions poetry and thinking would conceal themselves in beyng itself.

Poetry is *the presaging saga* [Vor-sage], it is the inceptual saga which appropriates itself as the favor bestowed by that which is not produced and that which cannot be calculated based on what is present to hand and actual. *Poetry is the favor of the guardian of the holy speaking her word in advance.*[45] Since poetry is presaging favor, there belongs to it the illuminating-projecting dimension of "fantasy." How are we to think the internal link between the task of poetry [*des Zu-dichtenden*] and the holy?

---

[45] {TN: Guardian (*Hüterin*) is gendered feminine.}

V. THE WORD AND LANGUAGE

cf. Contributions[46]
cf. On Mindfulness[47]
cf. Tutorials Summer Semester 1939[48]

108. The Word "of" Beyng

Is it ever possible for the word of beyng, the voice of the stillness of the offering, to keep "beings" "still?"

Since they are addicted to stimuli, beings desire noise. In need of tumult, they aspire to the public sphere and everywhere beings force the word into the vocabulary of language; beings evoke the illusion that one could inquire into the essence of the word in terms of a language created through vocabulary.

*

The awakening dream
Its gentle and quickening
fragrant airs
kindle
darker the night and fill it plumper with sagas.

*

You approached me as my greeting
– when in greeting you once again covered me with greetings
and wandered to the foot of the mystery
to which you have been bestowed.

109. Word and Language and Concept

The word at first appears as language – and all conversation gets objectified into language; and only after this object has been rendered common and comprehensible, does the investigation into the emergence

---

[46] Heidegger, *Contributions to Philosophy (of the Event)*.

[47] Martin Heidegger, *Mindfulness*, trans. Thomas Kalary and Parvis Emad (London: Continuum, 2006).

[48] Heidegger, *On the Essence of Language*.

of the object, along with the investigation into its components, achievements, and utility begin.

The fact that the word first appears as language is proper to the same history. This history bears all of the interpretation of beingness in its gradations, consolidations, and amalgamations. This history begins with the still unquestioned collapse of Ἀλήθεια, which is necessarily ungrounded. Metaphysics holds fast to the word as a structure language (φωνή σημαντική). In accordance with this metaphysical decision, everything that is referred to is transformed into a concept (in the representation of common sense (κοινόν)) – such concepts come to be as the circumscription of "word"-meaning. Consequently, "language" for its part is reduced to a logical-grammatical manner of thinking.

The reason why the doctrines of "concepts" and "logic" as such never live up to the philosophical "concept" can be found *in this*: the philosophical concept thinks – even when it thinks metaphysically – the beingness of beings in terms of *beings*, yet at the same time, it also thinks being. But being cannot be grasped in representational thinking – neither in *"ontological"* nor "ontic" thinking. Rather, being is only bespoken [*ersagen*] in the word "of" beyng. Saying of this kind never requires any justification or explanation, nor does it know anything of justification or explanation – certainly not justification and explanation in the form of proof. The word "of" beyng is never the reverberation or echo, nor is it the container of beyng, rather it is the essential prevailing of being itself. However, wherever there is talk of language as the reverberation of "being," there one refers to language as an attribute and one refers to the ringing out of the object and the ringing out of *beings*. An abyss of difference lies between the *word of beyng* and language as the echo of beings.

110. The Transition – Language and Word

The question is not: How do things stand with linguistics?

How do things stand with the philosophy of language?

Can there be a better and more originary inquiry here?

Language and metaphysics of language: at the most they are *as a whole* an impetus to a transition.

Metaphysics of language: λόγος – *human* – *beings as a whole* – φύσις – question of being.

The question is: *How do we stand to the word, what is the word capable of?*
How do we take the word?
The pseudo-power – the manner of speaking – using up – *vulgarization – uprooting.*
What is it? *A consequence of the abandonment of being.*
The abandonment in its culmination. It is unrecognized and yet dominant.
Nietzsche! → George – Rilke ‖ Hölderlin

111. Mediated Transitions from the Metaphysics of Language (Beyng-Historical) to Meditation "on" the Word

1. The unquestioned dimension in the metaphysics of language and that which is authentically said in the word: *beyng.*
2. Language – freedom – ground and abyss.
3. Saying and attending – as active silence.

Among all of this, there is an indication pointing to *Da-sein.*
Regarding the human and his essential transformation: he who is "borne" by the word – i.e. he who is attuned from the "voice" into the steadfastness required for the guardianship of the truth of beyng.

112. The Word

But also the word arising from saying – but from what is authentically said – the unsaid – that which is pre-served in silence [*Ver-schwiegene*]?!
But what, then, is sound – sounding?
Being and stillness – rupture in the appropriative event [*Er-eignung*] of strife.
Active silence [*Er-schweigung*] – what form does it take?
Rupture: it is not falling away [*Ab-fall*] and not privation, *rather essential prevailing* [Er-wesung] *of beyng.*

113. Metaphysics – Beyng-Historical Meditation

We are *not* asking for explanatory reasons (origin – provenance – of any sort), rather we are asking *about the abyssally grounded belonging or ex-pulsion into the abandonment of being proper to beings.*

That questioning gains a foothold in a questionless actuality and the questioning secures that actuality – and it thereby secures *itself* – through *explanation*.

Such questioning calls this actuality into question and inquires into the decisive encounter and into the necessity for the founding of the truth of beyng.

We nonetheless are the transition and we stand within the ambiguity. We stand *transitionally* within the abandonment of being. We stand within this: the hint of refusal and the concealed happening of the event [*Er-eignung*], or we stand within the culmination of the machination.

114. Language and Word

What stands in the purest defiance to itself is this: speaking "about" language" and maintaining beyng as the ground of the word in active silence. We must keep actively silent about the stillness of Da-*sein*. Active silence lies equidistant from both saying nothing and effusive chatter.

However, the fact that any form of the creative thinking of beyng must constantly express its essential prevailing leads thinking into the danger of discourse. If the world is not appropriated to it from the event of appropriation, then this discourse merely dissevers when it speaks.

115. Beyng and Word

Beyng is what is initially, constantly, and ultimately said, but as the *un*-said, to the extent that the beyng is never the object of a proposition, not even in the saying of the thinker. For this saying does indeed say beyng – but not in a stated proposition, rather it says beyng in be-speaking; what is said is understood comprehensively and it is the active silence of the happening of the event. Otherwise, unsaid being is pronounced in terms of beings and only in that way.

116. The Word "of" Beyng

The first thing that is said is the *unsaid*, i.e. *being*. It is said *from* being – of the *clearing* – it is said, and it *is* said – even though it is initially unsaid.

"God" – calling out, beckoning call.

This first element – is something which not only initially, ultimately, and constantly seeks to enter the *word* and seeks to *essence* as word to the highest degree, even if such a thing does not make it to our tongue or cross one's lips.

117. The Knowledge of the Word

The knowledge of the word stands in contrast to any form of the metaphysics of language. It might seem as if we could only reach this knowledge through an *incremental* deepening. That is what metaphysics knows as the authentic inner word – the "meaning," the "attribute"; But that would mean to assume that the external attribute of articulation should be sloughed off and the resonances and soundings should simply be forgotten in order to apprehend the purely non-sensible "spiritual" word; but all of that would simply be an intensified form of metaphysics.

What is required is something different – precisely the sounding out, the aspect of speaking bound to the mantra [*Spruchhafte*] must be known, but it must be known precisely not as "timbre [*Ton*]" and not as mere sensualization or utterance, rather it must be known as the mantra, as the rupture, as the earthing *of stillness*. It is the tolling out [*Er-klingen*] of stillness as the *preservation of beyng*, and the attunement of stillness is the attuning of attunement.

118. The Essence of the Word

We ask about the essence of the word, *not in terms of saying* and certainly not as a proposition (which for its part is taken as communication), rather the essence of the word as it arises from "listening." Yet this listening cannot merely be understood as attending, but instead as *the active silence of the happening of the event maintaining stillness*. This is the leap into the clearing of beyng, a clearing which belongs to the essential prevailing of beyng.

We must first let the essencing itself in its essentiality emerge from its origin, i.e. we must let it decide the *truth* of beyng for itself. A different attunement and posture of *essential knowledge* arises from that point.

But why does it arise out of active silence? Because saying also has its origin in active silence in the same way.

119. The Active Silence of Stillness

Only one "part" of the active silence of stillness is a way of attending, otherwise active silence is be-speaking – it is the saying of beyng as keeping silent.

At the same time, the *stillness* of beyng is the first word.

Yet the word is not regarded as an attribute (σημεῖον), nor as the meaning of beings, rather as the clearing of beyng.

120. Word and Fundamental Attunement – "Voice" and Sounding

The attuning essence of stillness – as the "voice" kept in silence. "Voice" here rings with the essential ambiguity of the *beckoning call* – but that is the ambiguity of the soundless call, and that is precisely the call which attunes authentically, i.e. the call which completes the displacement into the there.

Both fundamental attunement and its "voice" (beckoning call and displacement) open up the in-between in displacement.

Sounding is the essential consequence of stillness and is the "voice" of stillness, for stillness as the in-between endures the strife of world and earth. This strife as *rift* grants the first sound (regarded essentially). It *breaks* the stillness, but it precisely breaks stillness and then essences solely as a rupture and inter-ruption of stillness. This sounding is a privation of stillness.

121. Stillness

Stillness as the clearing of the there – the *first word*.
Keeping silent as *refusing preservation*.

122. Attending and Steadfastness in the There

Attending and steadfastness in the there are not to be regarded
as "listening" – perceiving with the ear –
rather as being-still: *being – stillness*.
But what is *stillness*? And of what sort is this "-being?" The being of there-being, *Da-sein*.

This would cause attending to lose its decisive reference to the *ear*, but also to lose mere *attention* [Auf-merken]. That form of sensibility and reasonability is not sufficient to bring about the culmination of Da-sein and to grasp Da-sein in its culmination: *being comprehensive.*

Subsequently, this form of sensibility and reasonability reveal themselves to be the unheeded foreground of Da-sein and the ultimate background of metaphysical questioning.

Attending: as *active silence* – active silence is not only prior to and beyond all sense perception, rather it is prior to and beyond all objects, but also prior to and beyond all beings and any form of customary comportment. The steadfastness in the clearing of beyng.

123. Attending – Perceiving – Reason – Da-sein

Listening and "listening";
Being able to listen: Hark! Be still – listen up – to what?
Keeping quiet – self-conjoining, placeholding, i.e. *attentive*
  ↓ [listening].

Active silence about the happening of the event (that means of beyng) – abyssal ground (of the surpassing ad-vent [*Über-kunft*]).
Grounding conjuncture into the bearing of encountering and strife.
Stead-fastness within the there.
Reason – arising from the attentiveness to beyng which maintains stillness; the leap into its truth (from the fundamental attunement of wonder); reason as a voice of this fundamental attunement.
But this origin – unquestioned, unexperienced and thus: only *a capacity within the animal!*

124. The Word of Failure

Speaking failure – that is the most abyssal encounter.
Such an encounter is entirely distinct from the essential prevailing of the word – the essential prevailing arising from beyng, i.e. from the happening of the event.

125. Language – Word

The One and the Other Projection

Statement and communication about beings.
Discourse – language – and vice-versa.

Call of beyng – actively silent; attuning into the steadfast be-speaking
of its truth.
Poetry – the mantra of the thinker.
"Obedient" to the event of appropriation.
Obedient – but this does not involve compliance to the *command*,
rather it involves leaping into the preserving truth of domination.

126. The Word

The word *as mantra* and before that it means the word as *active silence*
of the in-between.
But why, then, is there "sound?" Is it only because of com-munication?
But communication is *already* there in "attending."
So sound is only a confirmation of it? No!
Sounding and earth.
Sounding emerges from *the in-between* and emerges *from strife.*
Cf. Origin of the Work of Art[49]
Cf. Beyng[50]

127. The "Word"

The word is not an instance of attribution – which is the *objectivizing*
of beings.
The word is the *intoning of the clearing of beyng.*
It is not designation as furnishing with "name-signs,"
rather it is designation – as nom-ination [*Er-nennen*] to, *taking as,*
it is grounding leading into the clearing – com-mandeering – requisi-
tioning into the event.
Steadfast movement into the there.
"Self-consciousness" is a *consequence* of this, and self-consciousness
once again causes a slippage into the metaphysical domain.
Word – it arises from beyng,
Better said: beyng *essencing as the origin of the word* – active *silencing.*

---

[49] Martin Heidegger, "The Origin of the Work of Art," in *Off the Beaten Track*,
ed. Julian Young and Kenneth Haynes (Cambridge: Cambridge University Press,
2002), 1–56.
[50] Martin Heidegger, *Zum Ereignis-Denken*, vol. 73 of *Gesamtausgabe* (Frankfurt
am Main: Vittorio Klostermann, 2013).

128. The First Word

"Being" is the first word – but at first it is something actively silent, it is silence as authentic silencing.

And, *therefore*, being comes first, simultaneously and ultimately, in a countermanding force moving intimately into the saga.

Since stillness is the essence of the word, the first word is what is most thoroughly unsaid, it is what is undetermined in saying – *beyng*.

The word "of" beyng.

129. Word and Language

Language "is" in speaking. Speaking occurs as discourse. Discourse is history as conversation. The conversation is Da-sein. It is steadfast listening-in [*Er-hören*] (language "is" only in being bound to Da-sein and consequently – in accordance with the degree of concealment of Da-sein – it is ahistorical, an occurrence, something present-at-hand, a formation).

Da-sein is steadfastness within the active silence of the truth of beyng: active silence and listening. Active silence is the responsibility for the word.

The word is "of" beyng.

The word decomposes into something which is uttered in vocabulary words and sentences. The vocabulary and sentences are compiled together as a "language."

130. Language and Word

Language: the metaphysical interpretation of the "word."
λόγος as *ratio et oratio*.
    the "*et*" = and that means, and that culminates as
    reference to *oratio et ratio* – discourse and the "is" and essences as.
    Not "two" – rather *One* – the "One" of re-presentational, perceiving notation.
How?
But if *ratio* – νοῦς – λόγος are not sufficient for the foundation of
    the truth of being – rather they are only the first light cast upon
    beingness,
if *oration* and language are not first the sounding of declaration, rather
    they are the attuning and beckoning call leading into the event of
    appropriation,

then they are *the essential prevailing of the word* as the illuminating sounding of the active silence of the happening of the event directed into the in-between of the decision.

131. The Word

The word is the stillness of the rift. Beyng itself leaves behind the rift as the appropriating struggle of the event carried out between the encountering and strife. Beyng deposits this struggle into the abyss of clearing. Arising out of this, the word is capable of becoming – within the between of the countering force – the *conversation* and from there, in turn, it can become – within the between of world and earth – saga and proposition. Both tend to appear initially as audible articulation. Consequently, the representation of what we initially encounter as a human construct "arises" at this point. We misconstrue this to be a human tool (the animal present-to-hand and endowed with reason), taking it up to the most extreme point, the point at which one seizes on sound and articulation (φωνή) as primary and conjoins them as the "sign" to something signified, that is to say, one conjoins them to "meaning." This meaning then shows itself as something represented, which itself provides the directive to a being.

Because "sensible" and "nonsensible" present themselves here in the most immediately palpable form, i.e. because the word taken as language already introduces an essential misrecognition of the word based upon metaphysics, "logic" ends up usurping language. It then explains words and the connections between words through logic. This metaphysical entrapment of language, which is seized upon in its most immediately available form, delivers language over to grammar, logic, aesthetics, philosophy of language, and psychology. And, with the conception of language so thoroughly mired in misinterpretation, one then takes up the business of interpreting poetry. Hence it is also no accident that, in the culmination of metaphysics in Hegel, as well as in Nietzsche, the interpretation of the essence of language reaches the greatest shallowness and superficiality. The shallowness and superficiality are simply an essential consequence of the conflation of reason and language, that is to say, they are the essential consequence of the *ungrounding* of reason (i.e. ἀλήθεια as the truth of beyng).

132. The Attunement and the Calling

This involves calling to and calling out in the steadfast illuminating entrancing sense.

Fundamental attunements serve as the illuminating beckoning calls of the elevated listening [*Er-hörung*] of beyng as event of appropriation.

The word is this: *calling to beyng* as the active silence of the clearing of the abyss.

Language is *pronouncements about beings*.

Fundamentally different inceptions of the reference to saying.

Be-speaking ⇔ expression.

133. "Language"

(cf. Ponderings X)[51]

The origin of language arises from the word.

The word is heard as essential prevailing of beyng.

A *word – the decomposition of a word into "vocabulary"* – language speaks vocabulary.

Sounding – echo – or ringing-out *of the rift of the clearing* (attuning). Rift and call.

The still tolling out [*Er-klingen*] of the call of that rift in "sound" – whither and how is this? – "sounds" – mouth, tongue, throat, ear.

Why is it that language can only be a means of communication, why can it only be used and interpreted [?][52] as such?

The word – the mantra – is the sound of the clearing of the struggle between the countering force and strife.

VI. WORD AND "LANGUAGE"

134. Language

Metaphysical thinking "on" "language" (philosophy of language).

Beyng-historical thinking "of" language.

---

[51] Martin Heidegger, *Ponderings VII–XI, Black Notebooks 1938-1939*, trans. Richard Rojcewicz (Bloomington: Indiana University Press, 2017).

[52] {TN: included in the original.}

Beyng-historical thinking brings language to its essential prevailing as word, as the history of the grounding of truth of beyng.

The language "of" poetry; language "as" poetry (not to be confused with the romantic representation of "poesy" as "primordial language" – here the question of the origin is posed "*metaphysically*," in terms of an "explanation" of its emergence).

But this is not arbitrary "poetry" and this is not to be regarded as an object or domain of "cultural production" –
Hölderlin.

"Interpretation" – what does "interpretation" mean here? What does it call for?

135. The Word

The beckoning hint [*Zuwinkung*] of the stillness of the abyssal ground leading into the reticence of Da-sein.

This stillness sounds out within the human being. It sounds out as saga and as saying. It fades away into language and into what language speaks.

Where does this *sounding* come from? What form does it take?

It comes from the predominance of beings – from the presencing and preservation of beings.

Da-sein as keeping silent [*Ver-schweigung*] and authentic *conversation* within the in-between.

Conversation and saying.

Saying and expression.

Expression and speaking.

Speaking and that which is spoken (language).

136. Sound and Sounding and Beyng

A "sentence," a "word," a "passage" of a text – all of those things "*sound*" a certain way. That is, they mean something and signify something like this … Sounding of this sort does not mean ringing out or intoning. It does not mean that something "sounds [*hört*]" like this. Sound is grounded in "meaning" – but meaning is in the projection of beyng. This projection originates from steadfastness in the abyssal ground – steadfastness in the active silence of the happening of the event as the essential stillness of bearing.

Sound is the *reverberation* of stillness in the in-between of bearing-out. The "utterance" is not what is essential. The utterance is not the timbre which contains "meaning," yet it would also not be suitable to say that "meaning" is simply converted into timbre.

The word as a whole has its essential ground in beyng and it belongs to beyng – and therefore it can become a representation of beings as language and a representation of that which is spoken.

137. Animal – Human – Language

What is to be made of the cry and call as acoustic sound? Sound can also be grasped "abstractly" as acoustic sound.

The call and the cry of the woodpecker never "sound like [*lautet*]" something specific – rather they ring out [*klingt*] in such and such a way.

Cry and declaration and expression of the state of being carried along by the surrounding environment [Umgebungsbenommenheit] (neither "situations" nor "objects" when it comes to the animal, nor is it a matter of situational sound and objective sounds).

138. The Word

ζῷον λόγον ἔχον means: the animal which has the word.

It is not the *human* who "has" the word – rather, having the word makes the animal human.

"Having the word" here means: *possessing "language,"* φωνὴ σημαντική. σημαίνειν is signifying relating, gathering – λέγειν and this *in terms of re-presentation –*
gathering together ὄν *– qua* ἕν!

This is not only concerned with "language," rather it is concerned with language to the extent that language makes beings as such perceivable alongside language and makes the concerned *form of life into a perceptive one.*

The most internal and proper essential link between *word* and beyng, and hence the authentic essential grounding of the word, neither of those can be experienced anywhere here. Regarded from the standpoint of this link, it is nonetheless necessary to say:

The word "has" the human (not the lifeform), but this is the human as the *perceiver of beings* – re-presenting, per-ceiving (planning), *taking care.*

"To have" – refers to being decisively bound in the concealed essential ground – *bearing* within Da-sein and within determined attuning [*be-stimmend*] as *guardian of the truth of beyng.*

The beyng-historical mantra is this: the word has the human. Consequently, this mantra is fully and completely the reversal of the metaphysical sentence ζῷον λόγον ἔχον. The phrase: "the human has the word" consequently relinquishes everything to the metaphysical realm and leaves it undecided.

139. The Word

The "conversation" (cf. Hölderlin Lecture)[53]
– not the conversation as entertainment or as dialogue between an established "I" and "thou," and certainly not conversation in the Christian sense of man and God!

Rather, what is at stake is *conversation* as the sheltering of the word and as keeping silent. This is the happening of the event of the there as the play-space for the decision of the in-between.

140. The Word and the Human

The word belongs to the bearing-out as the event, which is directed toward the essence of beyng (active silence of the bearing). Only by dint of this assignation into the truth of beyng does "the human have the word," is "the word" up to him, does "the" decision rest with him, is the human bound to the decision and capable of language.

If the endowment of language is regarded from a physiological biological anthropological[54] perspective (which one takes as primary from the perspective of the *animal rationale*), then merely furnishing the human with the capacity for language has no significance at all for the meditation upon the essence of language. At most, it would only mean the complete blockage of any path leading into the meditation upon the essence. The entire "thrust" of facts, etc. arising from the historical analysis of language, from linguistics, and from the power of the habit of regarding language animalistically and "sentimentally" – none of that could do anything to ameliorate the complete blockage of the

[53] Martin Heidegger, *Elucidations of Hölderlin's Poetry*, trans. Keith Hoeller (Amherst, NY: Humanity Books, 2000), 56ff.
[54] {TN: Heidegger places the words in a series without commas or hyphens.}

essence of language. Arising alongside this experience of language and emerging from the same ground (namely the ground of metaphysics), is the "logical"-grammatical interpretation of language and the ground of all of its aesthetic psychological appendages.

The human is the "animal" which has the "word."
Word is meant here in an indeterminate and ambiguous manner as λόγος.
It means not only this: *gathering* – νοῦς – νοούμενον – ὄν
but also: *sounding* – φωνή – σημαίνειν.
Having the word = being constituted and equipped in such a way with the capacity for sounding and the capacity for the self-knowing perception of beings. The human as "a" being *among* the other non-"human" ones.

"Having the word" – if conceived of in a completely different sense: that the decision rests with the human, whether he merely belongs to beings (and beingness) and goes about his business there, or whether he risks the founding of the truth of beyng. The "word" – the essence of the decision here – is thought in terms of the being-historical essence of the word, i.e. it is not that the human "has" the word, rather that the word "has" the human.

The word belongs to the bearing, is in the encountering force: *"conversation,"* it is *naming* in conversational dispute and thus is in bearing out: naming conversation – grounding of truth – site of the there.

This creates the possibility of the essential enabling of the human. We initially always come across and regard the human metaphysically, reducing the human to something which is active in actuality and something which is present and *then* – remaining within the domain of metaphysics – we begin to explain the human based on first causes, be it "God" (*creator*), be it reason, be it "life."
Naming bound to the conversation as founding – the word of poetry.

141. The Word as Magic

The conception of the word as a "magical" apparition is merely the counterpart to the rational logical-grammatical conception of the word.

The animalistic – this involves captivated behavior and impact.

There is *lack of referentiality* [Un-bezogenheit] to beings as such in the genuine sense of animalistic privation. This applies as well to *"word," as well as what it "names,"* represents, and influences. It is equally so in the peculiar *lack of illumination of un-beings* [Un-seienden].

If one takes this as "more profound" by regarding it from the rational aspects of beingness, then that conclusion would correspond to the *fundamental*-character of animality – the dull, dark, and "instinctual" as the "*higher*."

1. this life itself is bound to the state of being carried out – "primitives"
2. one then produces a "doctrine" out of this, such as para-ontology and similar mindless trivialities.

VII. THE ESSENTIAL PREVAILING OF THE WORD

142. Beyng

Beyng "is" the clearing of "the" refusal. But the clearing does not essence as an opening. It is not the case that the refusal would then be what has been opened and is graspable objectively – but the clearing is also not a concomitant effect originating from the refusal, rather it is the entirety of the appellation known as the "clearing of refusal." It is the happening of the event of the event of appropriation [*Er-eignung des Er-eignisses*]. (Overcoming into the departure.) Yet refusal means keeping the bearings under self-restraint. Consequently, refusal holds the erupting conjuncture of the in-between up to the light.

Refusal does not state that beyng has withdrawn or that it is unrecognizable, and the refusal does not deem beyng "ir-rational" in the language of metaphysics. On the contrary: beyng as the clearing of refusal can be experienced in one way which, in contrast to what happens when we take recourse to the explanatory or to the enjoyment of what is observed "mystically," remains entangled only in the representation of something present. Beyng is neither merely "clearing," nor merely refusal, rather it is the self-appropriating clearing, it is the refusal (hesitation) illuminating within the clearing.

143. The Word "of" Beyng

The word is as word "of" beyng not simply as beyng's expression or sign. Rather, the word is the essential prevailing of beyng itself, and this essential prevailing *attunes* as event of appropriation. The stillness of the de-parture essences (the stillness of grace) in attuning.

The word is neither the word "about" beyng as the "object" "to be signified," nor is it the word "out of" beyng as its "subjective" "articulation" and appearance ("ex-pression"). The genitive in the word "of" beyng has a beyng-historical meaning – the word belongs in the preserving truth of beyng itself.

The word "attunes." It is not "about," nor "out of" anything. Beyng essences as the happening of the event of the clearing and that is the attuning of stillness.

144. The Word

The word is acquainted with stillness. The word's path is never laid at the level of what is spoken and calculated. The word is never simply the withdrawal from noise.

Only occasionally does the word chance upon a stalwart figure and attune him into Da-sein.

The word is dominance over the machination and this a dominance which does not require any power, and it reigns instead from the dignity of beyng, which happens as the event of appropriation, assuming its own rank. *Hölderlin's* Hymns [are] the first preliminary intimation of the active silence of the stillness of the bearing out. They lack any knowledge of the history of beyng and its moments. Hence, *thinkers* must arrive beforehand, thinkers as questioners, who become a source of incitement for all of the merely ostensible knowledge cloaked in the mode of representation.

145. The Word "Attunes"

The word attunes as something shifted into the clearing of beyng. Thus it is the first *reference* to the in-between – for every genuine word *says* "all." The genuine word elevates the strife between earth and world up to the point where it echoes back (in its intersection of countering) into the saga. And, therefore, the *spoken* word has many meanings [*vieldeutig*] in the sense of a "many" that is not a plurality, but is instead the unfathomable fissuring of beyng itself, in whose clearing beings "*are.*"

Word, the attuning as the voice of stillness, belongs to the word – whether or not the word is said and conjoined to what is said; How does such belonging arise out of beyng from the structure itself, and how does it essence within *beyng*?

146. Word and Language

The task is to consider word and language regarded from the stand-point of the word – the soundless voice of stillness – (word here is bound to the essence and is only the word "of" beyng) – by letting language fall back into the essential. Language cannot be refurbished, improved upon, and purified, for its history is grounded in the history of the truth of beyng.

Languages must collapse in the transition; a desolate neglect must empower itself with all of the noble words meant for rhetorical and literary use. Yet there will still remain a great amount of chatter among those who make the unthought desolation their business. They still must chatter away into the tumult of meaninglessness, for they are not permitted to have any intimation of the word of beyng. These people earn their wage as the servants of the machination. Even the semblance of disconsolation about the collapse of language cannot appear to them.

147. The Truth of the Word

The truth of the word is not to be determined in accordance with *adaequatio* and ὁμοίωσις, nor in accordance with correspondence, *calculation* and de-signation in terms of signs. The word constrains nothing through force, rather the word *sets free* in the essential sense that it – by attuning – first displaces us into the entuning clearing, into the free realm. *The word is the opening up of freedom.*

Only those who are free – the steadfast ones of Da-*sein* – can be attuned with voice [*ge-stimmt*] and can become listeners in the mode of those who are attuned [*als Gestimmte Hörende werden*].

The word liberates into freedom and, in order to preserve its essence, freedom seeks for itself the "law" in the sense of the conjuncture of what belongs in the illuminating circle of the particular freedom.

148. The Word of Beyng

The historical human, the human grounded in his essence upon a truth of beyng, is only a conduit for the word. Admittedly, he is a conduit for the word in such a way that even the human essences from the word alone, and within him is found the most inceptual conjuncture of the still clearing of the "in-between."

When will the orators [*Sagenden*] finally interpret an essential word as the word of being and carry out the voice of beyng in attunement, issuing a word incalculable in terms of what is known and what can be possessed, a word tolerating no idolization of language and shunning every utilization for discourse? All of this remains far removed from the essential clearing of the word. Within that clearing, beyng, which has been liberated to its essential prevailing, and beyng as such "is" the happening of the event: event.

149. The Active Silence of Stillness

Silencing: not saying something sayable, that means not communicating it; and this once again for different reasons (motivations and intentions).

Keeping silent: *wanting* to say something sayable, but not being able to (keeping silent out of an incapacity); leaving something ineffable in its unsayability (keeping silent based on a capacity). The unsayable and ineffable are each different from one another, for the "fitting" "word" is lacking; because what is thought has not been mastered; because it is not at all to be thought in the customary realm.

Active silence: the unsaid – because the unsaid is essential in all saying, coming to be as what is said in advance, emerging alongside and in the wake in its ground, and returning the ground of its unsaid state back to preservation and safeguarding, which protects from all saying, in order to maintain it in its ground.

This ground of this unsaid is the abyssal ground. Beyng itself essences as the abyssal ground.

Active silence does not arise from the insufficiency of discourse, rather it arises from belonging to stillness and a belonging intended for stillness.

In its inceptual form the word is the voice of stillness held in active silence.

Stillness is then the abyssal ground of the appropriative event.

Active silence itself is occasionally – in moments of transition – obligated to enter into saying, but this saying does not break the stillness, rather it only attests that the stillness is not capable of compelling what is kept actively silent, for silence must be appropriated from stillness.

150. The "Essence of the Word" – Stillness

(i.e. its essential prevailing)

The word "of" beyng is neither a subjective nor objective genitive – rather?

The essence of the word: stillness as voice – attuning beckoning call – attuning voice of stilling stillness (re-fusal of the abyssal ground from the happening of the event of bearing out) – *"voice" from attunement* as the opening displacement leading into the there.

and *only therefore can language* appear as verbal articulation.

Rupture of stillness – *this rupture* from *the rift and strife (the strident word).*

Beforehand: *attuning stillness.*

"Stillness": initially conceived as lack and as a way of sounding and as movement, hence conceived in terms of *noise* and *dis-quiet.*

But what about the other way around? Is that only a reversal?

Or is it *of a different* essence, is it essential prevailing?

"Sounds" as sounding are not the *lack* of stillness, rather they are *its* rupture and are thereby *an active essential prevailing* [Er-wesung] *(of the event) into the open.*

151. Stillness

Stillness
without movement – sitting still, calm in the air,
without a sound.
keeping still, being still, "stilling": *hunger and thirst.*
Stillness: being gathered together, restraint, *"anguish."*
Sheltering, quiet, coming to a halt.
Stillness: neither from privation of sound nor at all merely a privation.
Stillness: the over-flow of the abyssal ground.
Overflow out of and as failure – refusal.
Stilling: bringing to silence; to quiet, *to gentleness.*
Stillness and nursing – gently bringing to rest.
("He stilled the stone," Stifter, "Description of the Little Fir")[55]

---

[55] Adalbert Stifter, "Der beschriebene Tännling," in *Gesammelte Werke in Sechs Bänden*, vol. 2 (Wiesbaden: Insel-Verlag, 1959), 637–692, 682.

152. Stillness

The *essencing word* as attuning stillness (the still word).
The *disputatious word* as *saga*, as verbally articulated *sound* [*Ver*laut*barung*].
The still and *disputatious* word each united in different ways.
The *disputatious* is not already a corrupted essence and is also not "expression" of something "internal," for the essential stillness is the stilling down [*Er-stillung*] of *the outside* – of the opening of the clearing. "Inside" is always merely *external*!

153. Beyng and Word

Word as word of beyng,
Being – truth of being,
projecting leaping in,
Da-*sein*.
Active silence of beyng – also not like "bringing" being "to language." But active silence is not "nothing" and it is distinct from the unsaid as previously conceived, for that mode of the unsaid only refers to beings – echoing the forgetting of being.
The active silence and the fundamental attunement.

154. Beyng

In failure [Ver-sagung] *beyng bestows its truth*:
stillness – as attuning opening *displacement* into the clearing of the self-concealing.
   In the bestowal of truth beyng appropriates the departure.
As happening of the event, beyng grounds its essential prevailing as bearing.

155. Word and Language

If the word – is the word "of" beyng, then only in terms of the truth of *beyng* relating to the other *word* and thus transformation of the reference "to" "language" – no longer thinking "about" the word, nor about language – rather?
Directives.

VIII. IMAGE AND SOUND – THE SENSIBLE

Language
Differentiation
Anguish

156. Not Thinking Without Images

Not thinking without images,
rather *thinking out of the simple images and back into these simple images.*
Image – the gaze conjoining itself (pliantly) into the hint.
The sparsity of the simple image.

157. Anguish

That we have not yet been made aware of the *sensible* –
that we still represent it errantly and do not yet *think* it.
Already the appellation alone is *errant* – for it alludes to the perceived, the *sensed*.

158. The Inceptual Element of "the Sensible" Bound to the Event

(sensible-non-sensible, sound – anguish)
The *sensible* is "more sensible" than metaphysics thinks:
   it is more earthy – *more sheltering – more inceptual;*
the *non-sensible* is more "super-sensible" than metaphysics thinks:
   it is more illuminating – more unconcealing – *more inceptual.*
Why does the "differentiation" take hold here? How does the human *establish* himself within that differentiation as the unexperienced and inceptionless open realm? This involves solidification through τέχνη – εἶδος – ὕλη.

The *sensible is regarded* as *affection* and stimulus, *"arousal"* and desire –
   Lack of desire; *dull* – signless; *mere hustle or tumult or busyness.*
The *earthly:* sheltering the open, calling to heaven and the first ring dance of the event along with it.
   The *foreign* is the first thing to be thought in this way – the self-fulfilling sheltering of the beloved – sheltering of the greeter.

159. Imageless Thinking –

Imageless thinking is
impossible,
what is bound to the image – but how to differentiate it from the *poetizing* image?
The word and the image –
the essence of the *image –*
the gaze conjoining itself, conjoining into the hint,
peering in. The image and the sensible.
Beyng only becomes beyng in encouragement – as the word to the human.
The word appropriates the human.

*

Inceptual thinking:
"non-ekstatic" ekstasis,
not enthusiastic ekstasis.

IX. LANGUAGE

160. Language

The conversation of the saga of beyng is the *conjuncture* of releasing
preserving-dwelling serenity leading into freedom [*Freyheit*],[56]
it is the fortress, the inconspicuous, the sheltering of the guardians of
the event.
Juncture of dwelling.
Fortress of anguish.

161. [Questions on Language]

1. How – in what way is *language* experienced for us? What and how is
   language?
2. How is language – general linguistics – thematized here?
   In which regard and based on what intention is it objectified?
3. To what extent has "language" drawn us *into reflection*?
   Has something become worthy of questioning?
4. Our experience of language and the *Greek world* – "logic" –
   "grammar."
   Once again: the Greek world, *the pre-Platonic*.
5. Spoken and written language – *writing*.
   Language is always the speaking of a conversation.
   The conversation is the answer to the word of the saga of beyng.
   The answer as the poetry of the saga.
   Poetry as indicator – σῆμα θῆμα, sentence – saga, letting beings be
   present and absent,
   Saga of beyng.

Language
Sentence – Word
Saga
Beyng
(Event)

The sanctuary of dwelling of the fateful human being,
Building upon this sanctuary.

---

[56] Correlating to the antiquated spelling of *beyng*, Heidegger renders freedom
(*Freiheit*) using the antiquated spelling *Freyheit*.

The sentence – grammatical concept *for the original simple unity of language*.

A piece or the *entire language*?

How is the isolation of this unity to be understood?

The expression of language *contained within itself, a saga*.

"*My* lords(?)!" – "My *lords(?)*!"[57]

1. "Sentence" is a structured unit of expression (*pluit*)
2. "He couldn't get past the first 'sentence'."
3. The "*principle* [*Satz*]" of non-contradiction

λόγος (Aristotle, Dionysius Thrax): a discourse [*Rede*] – a saga, λόγον ἔχον: discourse, "language"

sententia

annuntiatum

phrase- thèse

Λόγος as ἀπόφανσις pro-position [*Aus-sage*],

λόγος – gathering, unification of ἔν in λόγος:

1. saying from the matter, manifesting it
2. about the subject
3. communication – speaking out

Is the form of the stated proposition [Aussagesatzes] *the form of human discourse as such?*

Hölderlin writes these introductory words intended for the draft of an essay about the historical epochs of the Occident:

"For us everything focuses on the spiritual,

We've become poor in order to become rich." III, 621 (Hellingrath)[58]

Language and *sign* – sign-ification [*Be-zeichnung*] – indicated meaning.

"Sign-tool" first as indicator – worlding of world – event to memory, hence "language" is not to be thought from the standpoint of *signum* and *signal*.

---

[57] {TN: Heidegger uses the common phrase "*Meine Herren*," which is simply the common address for "gentlemen," for example when calling the attention of an assembled crowd (of men). While the first form Heidegger uses above indicates an inquisitive stance, the second form indicates a more politely commanding way of calling a group's attention. *Herr* bears the meanings of "lord," "master," "gentleman," but also the title "Mr."}

[58] Friedrich Hölderlin, *Sämtliche Werke, Historisch-kritische Ausgabe*, ed. Norbert von Hellingrath, Friedrich Seebass and Ludwig von Pigenot (Berlin: Propyläen-Verlag, 1943), 621.

Hence a circle – but not accidentally; origin of the circle?
Provenance of the signs from association and *appointment*!

Function of *meditation* – bringing back once again to a middle point,
uni-versal.
Thinking and poetry
Language and craft of language [*Sprachwerk*]
Art and the work of art [*Kunstwerk*] –
everything in the course of history, historical memory of what is past
Reception of *what is coming*
The *style* of *preparation and meditation* of those *free of need.*
Hölderlin – Language: the sanctuary of the essence of the historical
human within beyng.

X. LANGUAGE

162. Remark

On Hamann's dictum: "Reason is language, λόγος."[59]
If λόγος is to be thought in Heraclitus' sense, then this dictum says: gathering together, sheltering – namely: the gathering together of what is present into the Oneness of presence. Yet Hamann's interpretation (in line with the Gospel of John) can be set aside here.

More essential here is the question of why "reason" is named. Reason stands for the perception of beings in their being, the perception of objects in their objectivity; this is the state of being received in reason. It is reason. The being of beings, their beingness, is reason. This remains the case, even if this realization does not come to light. Determined by the difference of beings and being, reason remains attuned to this difference. Yet this difference appropriates itself within the dif-ferentiation for world and thing. Dif-ferentiation appropriates itself as the tolling sound of stillness. This tolling is the speaking of language. Within all of this unthought there essences in concealment what Hamann has in mind when he says: reason is language. Hamann was not able to think any of that; he nonetheless peered into the abyss of language.

Hamann's dictum gives a hint toward the concealed reference of language to the essence of beyng in terms of difference itself.

163. λόγος

Meditation in questioning is once again necessary: how did λόγος reach the meaning of saga and discourse?
λέγειν – (Cf. Heraclitus Lecture 1943 and 1944)[60] – reading – gathering.
Gathering what is present into presence –
presence gathering into itself out of Ἀλήθεια –
yielding-forth and thus illuminating – sheltering in unconcealment, gathering the one together with the other – *holding-together*: Ἐόν – Λόγος.
Consequently: λέγειν – as ὁμολογεῖν (Heraclitus, Fragment 50)[61]

[59] Johann Georg Hamann, Letter to Herder, August 10, 1784, in Johann Georg Hamann, *Schriften*, ed. Friedrich Roth, vol. 7 (Leipzig: G. Reimer, 1825), 151.
[60] Heidegger, *Heraclitus*.
[61] Diels and Kranz, vol. 1, p. 161, 22 B 50; see also the lecture from 1951: Martin

Λέγειν is saying – not out of audible articulation, rather *from the co-responding gathering* of the inceptually upsurging gathering. It is audible articulation out of the reference to the presence of what is present – (from the perspective of a *preservation* that is still unthought and inceptually unthinkable).

Collected presence [das Gewese][62] – as the gathering of presencing [*An-wesens*].

Heidegger, "Logos" (Heraclitus, Fragment B 50), in *Early Greek Thinking*, trans. and ed. David Farrell Krell and Frank A. Capuzzi (San Francisco: HarperCollins, 1984), 59–78.

[62] *Gewese* has at least four distinct meanings: (1) estate, landholdings, property (2) affectation (3) ado, fuss (4) the verbal substantive of *wesen* ("to essence"). I have selected the final one of these, though there are clearly multivocal resonances in Heidegger's use of the term.

On Eduard Mörike's Poems
"September Morning"
and "At Midnight"

September Morning (1827)

In fog *rests still* the world,
woods and meadows still dreaming:
Soon you'll see, *when* the veil falls,
The blue sky undisguised,
In autumn vigor the muffled world
Flowing in warm gold.

At Midnight (1827)

Serenely the night mounted the land,
It leans dreaming on the mountain's wall
Her eye now *sees* the golden scales
Of time at rest in the *same* plates
   And the springs roar forth bolder
   They sing of mother, of the night, in the ear
   Of the day
   The day that was today.

The ancient old lullaby,
She notices nothing, has grown weary of it;
The sky's blue sounds even *sweeter* to *her*,
Of the fleeting hours of the yoke swinging *equally*.
   Yet the springs always *retain* the word
   Slumbering the waters sing on
      Of the day,
   Of the day that was today.

This evening I would like to enter into conversation with you. Conversations like this are always a matter of luck. For the proper conversation also depends less on one's agility in speech and more on the care and duration of listening.

Alas, today's attempt at a conversation is especially *risky*.

For this conversation breaks in – or so it seems – from the *outside* and arrives *unmediated* into the orderly course of your studies.

There is nonetheless a *specific point of contact* with *the pedagogy of German language instruction*. In your German classes you learn about grammar, orthography, and reading – you also learn about the structure of the language, and about writing and reading. You also learn how to listen to what is spoken and written. This pedagogy is concerned with how the youth are supposed to be educated into the proper use of their *mother* tongue.

We grow into our *mother* tongue. Or, better said, we grow out from our mother tongue – as if we were sprouting from a *root* into the full maturity of life. The mother tongue is so *commonplace* and so *near* that it is difficult for us to attend to the language itself.

As a result, we are prone to *mis*recognize the *power and plentitude* of the language.

Herder once said of the mother tongue (*On Recent German Literature*)

"A mountain, in comparison to a small number of philosophical abstractions, a molehill artificially built up – a few drops of extracted spirit in comparison to the vast expanse of the ocean!"[63]

The *everyday* use of language *serves* to facilitate *comprehension* between people, that is to say, it serves communication. This *conception* of language *is being taken to an extreme* these days. We barely take note of this process and we fail to measure its impact. You know that today they are not only building machines for computing, but also machines for thinking and translating (language machines) as part of their project to construct electronic brains.

None of this is at all outlandish anymore and it is not simply an arbitrary exaggeration. The modern form of understanding and the modern way of providing notification is *building up* to the development

[63] Johann Gottfried Herder, *Über die neuere Deutsche Litteratur. Fragmente*, in *Sämtliche Werke*, vol. 2, ed. Bernhard Suphan (Berlin: Weidmannsche Buchhandlung, 1877), 98.

of these machines. The construction of such machines is only possible because one already conceives of language as *an instrument of information and nothing more than* an instrument of communication. *The human being's relation* to language is undergoing an *uncanny transformation*. This transformation is occurring amid a state of *total calm*.

In contrast to this, the discovery and employment of *atomic energy* – for whatever purposes it may be intended – is a *very crude affair*, which is playing out in the *peripheral areas* of our existence [*Daseins*].

By touching on these things, I in no way intend to pass any value judgment on this *process*. It is only necessary to call attention to it. This reference provides an *occasion*, as if it had arisen of its own accord, to *contemplate how* things stand in our *relationship* to language – and thus to contemplate *how* things stand with *language itself*.

This much remains *indisputable*: Language is a means of communication.

Language serves that role *everywhere in the everyday*, and wherever one deals with *habitual relations*.

But there are also *other* relations which are beyond the *habitual* ones –

Goethe calls them simply "*deeper*" relations and he says this of language:

"We get by in life with our *everyday* language, for we describe *only* *superficial* relationships. The instant we speak of *deeper* relationships, *another* language springs up: *poetic language*."[64]

Goethe distinguishes everyday language from poetic language. Because deeper relations are involved in drawing that distinction, *there is reason to hope* that we will also reach *deeper* into the *essence and reign* of language by *passing through poetic* language.

That is why I have selected two *poems* for our conversation today.

The choice of the poet Eduard Mörike might at first seem *arbitrary*, much like the choice of the two poems might seem arbitrary.

Only the selected *poems* themselves are capable of *justifying* the choice. The two poems bear these titles:

"September Morning" and "At Midnight"

[64] Johann Wolfgang von Goethe, "Symbolism," in *Scientific Studies*, vol. 12 of *Goethe Edition*, ed. and trans. Douglas Miller (New York: Suhrkamp Publishers, 1988), 26.

Both originate from the same year (1827), though Mörike's poems were first published in 1838.

For now let us simply read the poems; "simply" – that means to read them unmediated and in such a way that we leave behind the *many concerns* which have already cropped up.

Poems! What are poems good for anymore? *Where* do poems belong? And, especially, what does it all mean to speak *about* poems? – Doesn't this always inevitably end up just being endless droning on?

If anything at all is to come of our conversation, then we ought to "experience" the poems. The "experience" is most likely to occur when you have the chance to read them undisturbed and to yourself – in a moment which compels you to pick up a volume of poetry.

But now – now it seems we are just haggling about "poems."

So let us set aside our concerns for now. And let us simply read the first poem.

"September Morning"

We have read and understood everything –;
It contains no language other than the customary one –; yet perhaps a single phrase jumps out – a phrase at the beginning of the penultimate line of the verse: *"in autumn vigor"* –
Vigorous in the manner of autumn.
1. full of vigor – culminated – "ripe"
   fruits
2. sheltering power concealed within it – seeds –
   promises – the coming blooms
   And in the same verse, *perhaps yet another* word jumps out.
"muffled" – a certain interplay with "autumn vigor"
"muffle" – "to create smoke" – *to temper* the fire
sprouting and blooming, the opulence of summer.
"retrieved"
"subdued," and thus more thoroughly capable – "vigorous."

   "September Morning"
"in warm gold"
Gold – | *warm*   glowing – warming – splendor – resplendence
           Bringing – preserving – resting
                   Cf. Pindar, Isthmian Odes V
                   Μᾶτηρ Ἀλίου πολυώνυμε Θεῖα,
                   σέο ἕκατι καὶ μεγασθενῆ νόμισαν
                   χρυσόν ἄνθρωποι περιώσιον ἄλλων.

> Mother of Helios, Θεῖα the many-named;
> for your sake men have made the great strength of
> gold
> to be a thing prized above other possessions.[65]

To read – what does it mean *to read?* It means to gather word for word.
It means to gather together around what is said –
to gather around the unsaid

   What does the poem say! |
There is the *description* of nature on one side and man on the other side
"Propositions" –   *"expressing emotions"*
Title: "Time of Year and of the Day" | *September* – Autumn
(Way of writing!)   ↑   *Dwindling* of the
                              ↓   year
                 Morning: Rising
                           Dawn

Which saying is involved here? "No propositions"
endowed: *rising of the autumnal day*
The entirety of the poem   "brought to language"
                                into language
its "totality?!"   as language concealed.

The second poem
"At Midnight"
Title – center of time – |*"time itself"* |

The structure of the poem in its written form.
Two stanzas of 8 lines each.
Each time: 5th and 6th lines indented in;
   the 7th line only three words: "of the day"
   set further in.
   The 8th line loops back – but now it returns:
more clearly: *against* the night. | center of time |
the ephemeral – | *always returning back* |

---

[65] Pindar, "Isthmia V," in *The Odes of Pindar*, trans. Richmond Lattimore (Chicago: University of Chicago Press, 1947), 139.

The arbitrary element interchanging at each moment – one and the same
     "monotonously" *lulling to sleep*
     in contrast the sustaining verses – 3 and 4.
     night as midnight
     "sees" – "*hears*"! "sounds even *sweeter* to her"!
     blue of the sky   the blue of the night as mother
                    the blue of the day   middle
the golden scale | "*same* plates" – yoke sweeping *equally*
     \   /
     of time | "balanced" into stillness

Poems – | endowed saga – |
Endowing – calling forth
     grounding
     bestowing
     building (establishing) the *dwelling* of the human
the perduring element: the enduring – guaranteeing – unexpectedly
entering –
inexhaustible – (the same)
saga – "language?"
poems – where do they belong? What is the place of the poem?
the poem has been
transformed into literature – into the written word.
previously – song – word and manner
for celebrating lofty life – of society –
now – out of use –
"the absolute poem" – Goethe!
the spontaneity of the unique palpitation of the heart.
|| the saying itself *singing*!

What is language? What happens in speaking about language!
Talking about poems.

And yet!
out to sea – retreating back to the familiar shore
traditional conception – "grammar"
                    "logic"

W. v. Humboldt (Herder-Hamann)

"The human is human through language; but in order to invent language, he already had to be human."
On the Comparative Study of Language 1820[66]

"Language is world-outlook."[67]
"impression of the mind and the world-outlook of speakers."[68]
"... a true world which the mind must insert, by its own inner labour, between itself and objects."[69]

Language as energeia and ergon
Humboldt German Idealism | Kant – Leibniz |

All speaking about – taking back –
Relinquishing the poems to their "form"
Gathering of the re-mittance [Zu-stellens]
of the "enduring" (event)

Astonishment –
learning to be surprised – in the face of the secret of the inconspicuous.
Language – saying – *the most proximal and near.*
The approaching path is the most remote one.

---

[66] Wilhelm von Humboldt, *Über das vergleichende Sprachstudium in Beziehung auf die verschiedenen Epochen der Sprachentwicklung*, in *Sprachphilosophischen Werke Wilhelms von Humboldt*, ed. Heymann Steinthal (Berlin: Dümmler Verlagsbuchhandlung, 1883), 51.

[67] {TN: Quote attributed to Wilhelm vom Humboldt, *Über die Verschiedenheit des menschlichen Sprachbaues und ihren Einfluß auf die geistige Entwicklung des Menschengeschlechts*, in *Sprachphilosophischen Werke Wilhelm's von Humboldt*, ed. Heymann Steinthal (Berlin: Dümmler Verlagsbuchhandlung, 1883), 287f. The precise formulation cannot be found there.}

[68] {TN: The quote is misattributed and misstated in the original text. I have inserted the correct version. Wilhelm von Humboldt, *Über den Dualis* (Berlin, Druckerei der Königlichen Akademie, 1828), 20.}

[69] Wilhelm von Humboldt, *On Language: The Diversity of Human Language-Structure and its Influence on the Mental Development of Mankind*, trans. Peter Heath (Cambridge: Cambridge University Press, 1988), 157.

Appendices

1.

Humboldt, "On the Comparative Study of Language 1820"[70]
Steinthal p. 51

"The human is human through language; but in order to invent language, he already had to be human."

"Language must ... rest entirely and already in its nexus in the human being."[71]

————

"In short, language is the mark of our reason, by which alone it acquires and propagates forms." Herder[72]

2.

Herder: *poesy* is the *primordial language* of humanity.
But what is *poesy*?

3.

Every endowment is inexhaustible.

[70] Humboldt, *Über das vergleichende Sprachstudium*, 51.
[71] Ibid., 51. Heidegger has modified the quote slightly.
[72] Johann Gottfried von Herder, *Outlines of a Philosophy of the History of Man*, trans. T. Churchill (New York: Bergman Publishers, 1966), 234.

Addenda

Image and Word

The *topic* of the seminar is *circumscribed* by the title: *Image and Word*. An indication is at first necessary in order for us to avoid any detours, if it is at all possible to avoid them, but also in order for us to avoid preempting the matter at hand, but instead to let the conversation itself arrive at the matter. This indication is *at first* sufficient to point out what is supposed to grant the conversation *its necessary motivation* in *each respective case*. We will take the *guiding threads* for the seminar from *five* areas that seem to lie far apart from one another. These areas are:

1. From Augustine, *Confessions*, Book X, sections 7 and 8[73]
2. A sketch from "the experience of thinking"[74]
3. From Zhuangzi's "Mastering Life"[75]
4. Paul Klee's 1924 Jena lecture "On Modern Art"[76] – main thoughts
5. Heraclitus, Fragment 112.[77]

---

[73] Augustine, *Confessions*, trans. R. S. Pine-Coffin (London: Penguin, 1961).

[74] Martin Heidegger, "Aus der Erfahrung des Denkens," in *Aus der Erfahrung des Denkens*, vol. 13 of *Gesamtausgabe* (Frankfurt am Main: Vittorio Klostermann, 2002), 75–86; translated as "The Thinker as Poet," in *Poetry, Language, Thought*, trans. Albert Hofstadter (New York: HarperCollins, 2001), 1–14.

[75] Zhuangzi, "Mastering Life," in *The Complete Works of Zhuangzi*, trans. Burton Watson (New York: Columbia University Press, 2013), 299–300.

[76] Paul Klee, *On Modern Art* (London: Faber and Faber, 1966).

[77] "Thinking well is the greatest excellence and wisdom: to act and to speak what is true, perceiving things according to their nature." Heraclitus, "Fragment 112," in *The Art and Thought of Heraclitus: An Edition of the Fragments with Translation and Commentary*, trans. Charles H. Kahn (Cambridge: Cambridge University Press, 1979), 43.

One would be perfectly *well* justified in thinking that a *single one* of these guiding threads would be *extensive* enough to take up the few hours available to us, if we were to follow it with even a small degree of meditative reflection.

But the aforementioned threads are so peculiarly *interwoven* with one another that a *weave* [*Gewebe*] becomes visible within them and this is a weave which reveals a collected essence [*Gewese*], which we otherwise *would not be able to* catch sight of.

(We are addressed by it from very far away through the title "Image and Word.")

The necessarily *peremptory* pursuit of these five threads may *at the same time* become an *occasion* to meditate further on the interweaving *in the future*! This requires contemplating how a weave is a veil which uncovers by covering, covering the imageless element of the wordless.

The *preparation* for the individual lessons does not primarily involve knowledge of the aforementioned texts. It instead relies more on a *gathering into the capacity* to listen to one another, i.e. a capacity to perceive what the individual text in each case is precisely *not* capable of *saying*.

Such a gathering demands a *preparation* for the *mysterious* element of the matters at hand and for the states of affairs which approach [an-*gehen*] us in the conversation.

The *style* of such a conversation cannot be described in advance. Instead, the style must constitute itself *out of the matter*, and do so according to the measure of *how* we are approached [an-*gegangen*]. *In the process*, we may come to realize that we are already released *into* the matter.

Since the urgent questions which confront us are manifold, while the number of hours remains limited, *incursions* into the texts cannot be avoided, and likewise a certain *pedagogical* practice cannot be avoided.

From the outset, this demands – or so it at least seems – that we have clear statements prepared in advance in order to explain what is meant by the title: What does image mean? What does word mean?

If we intended to answer these questions by following *along the tracks of definitions*, then we would obstruct our *path* into the *conversation* by taking that very approach.

But luckily – for it is so destined – we already *understand* what the names say, even if this *understanding* rests upon opinions that remain untested, and even if these opinions remain blended together in an *indeterminate* state.

More important than the *alacrity* in the *manipulation* of definitions, which is a way of thinking that only feigns the semblance of rigorous thinking, *is that, in the midst of our examination* and elucidation of the topic "Image and Word," we must remain aware that we are standing squarely in the middle of the plight of our world age and that we are not dealing with minor matters or merely dallying in aesthetic affairs [*Dinge*].

The *essential transformation* of the image and word – and the essential transformation of the *human relation* to both – does not just arise from a recent perplexity, nor does it arise from the resultant *consumption* of word and image; the transformation referred to above is carried out for its own sake through *im*pulses [An*treiben*] whose essential provenance one chooses to look away from.

Hence, in the course of the conversation, even if there is no recognizable definition of image and word, we all are nonetheless compelled to *clarify the domain* into which both names speak.

Yet an approximate *indication* is necessary to clarify these domains. This indication serves to point out the *direction* of the path which the conversation would like to take.

Part Two

On the Question of Art

On the Question of Art

Let us attempt, in all due brevity, to say a few things about the question of art. The questions are merely suggestions; they are simply thoughts offered for contemplation; they provide the impetus for a possible conversation on the evening of this festive day.

Presumably, there has never before been such a bewildering array of things spoken and written about art as there is in the current moment. There must be some reason to account for this. We discover one of these reasons as soon as we contemplate the fact that, in the age of Greek art, there was no such thing as literature about art. The works of Homer and Pindar, Aeschylus and Sophocles, the buildings and sculptures of the great masters, they all spoke for themselves. They spoke because they had their place within the whole of the existence of this astonishing people. The art of the sculptors, for example, required no exhibitions, and needed no documentation. Only when the great age of Greek poetry and plastic arts began to reach its end did Aristotle utter a word about art. That word has been forgotten and, as a result, it has not yet been sufficiently thought through. Later, in the concluding remarks, I will touch on this word of Aristotle briefly.

For now, let me call attention to the fact that today it is precisely the visual arts (the formation of the Greek polis in the face of the gods and the planning of space in the 20th century are admittedly two fundamentally different epochs of Occidental existence [...]),* and above all the plastic arts, which are once again assuming a place of prominence. They are entering into a new relation to the industrial landscape, and are integrating themselves into architecture and city planning. These fields have a say in the planning of space. This is evidently due to the

---

* [This is followed by a few indecipherable stenographic signs.]

fact that the visual and plastic arts have a pronounced relationship to space and they comprehend this engagement as a certain kind of engagement with space.

What is space? What does engagement with space mean in this context? Who is at all supposed to answer these questions for us? Perhaps one could offer the assurance that the artist is the one who is best informed about these matters. *The artist* executes the engagement with space. Certainly. But can the sculptor as sculptor, for example, communicate through a plastic work what space is and what engagement with space means? Never. He can communicate that just as little as the physicist as physicist can say what physics is by communicating in the mode of physics and with the tools of physics. What physics is cannot be examined *physically*. Physics is not a potential object for a physics experiment. What the visual arts are, and what art as such is, those are things which cannot be defined by means of a chisel and hammer or a paint and brush, but they also cannot by defined with the aid of a work produced by means of those tools.

Here we stumble across a curious state of affairs. How difficult it will be to grasp this problem can be elucidated with a proposition which a renowned art connoisseur and author was recently heard to say: "Art is what is made by significant artists." Lovely. But let us ask in response to that: Who is an artist? Evidently, it is he who satisfies the claim of art. And who is a significant artist? It is not the artist most often traded and sold, rather the artist who satisfies the highest claim to art. And what is art? Answer: art is what significant artists make. We're spinning around in a circle. And the art connoisseur's proposition about art rings hollow. Neither does it say anything about art, nor about artists. But this circular movement of representation is no accident. We encounter it everywhere. When we say: Space is what the sculptor engages with, then the question immediately arises: Who is a sculptor? Answer: the sculptor is an artist who engages with space in his own way.

How do we find our way out of this circle? Answer: We cannot get out of it at all. Who is this we? We humans. Hence this spinning around belongs to us as human beings. Instead of making the futile attempt to come out of this circle, the task is to experience what state of affairs we are dealing with when we come across this circle again and again.

We only become ripe for this experience through forebearing and manifold reflection. For the moment, however, a hint will suffice. We will attempt to follow it with an eye toward this question: *What is space?* We find the first thematic elucidation of this question in Book IV of Aristotle's lectures on φύσις. One translates this primordial Greek word very imprecisely by the Latin *natura* – nature.

By φύσις, the Greeks mean what is present, and what is present and appears of its own accord. This stands in contrast to what is present and only owes its presence to production by humans, i.e. τέχνη; τέχνη is also the Greek name for what we call art.

In his lecture about φύσις, Aristotle names what we call space with two different words: τόπος and χώρα. Τόπος is the space which a body immediately fills up. This space occupied by the body is first of all constituted by the body, σῶμα, and this space in turn has the same limits as the body. This space is simultaneously the place of the body.

In contrast, χώρα refers to the space which can, as it were, receive and envelope the space, δεκτικόν – περιέχον. In the Greek sense, when regarded from the perspective of the body, space is the place of the body. Every body has its own place; the light bodies up above, the heavy ones down below. Space has designated places.

Later, in modern physics, space loses this characterization. It becomes pure, uniform three-dimensional extension as the terrain for the movement of points of mass. Kant then interprets space from the perspective of the body as a way in which the human as a subject existing for itself intuits the objects which encounter it in advance.

In Greek thinking and in modern thinking, space, even given all the differences in the manner of thinking, is conceptualized from the perspective of bodies. Space is three-dimensional extension (*extensio*), within which bodies and their movements take their course – their *stadion*, where they stroll around.

στάδιον and strolling [*spazieren*] (span) are the same word as *spatium*. *Extensio*, extension and *spatium*, span – that we call space. It is represented as the container for bodies.[1]

According to the customary mode of representing space, the human also stands and moves like a body at rest or in motion with its volume in space.

But what then is space itself in its own property as itself? What grants space the possibility of taking on the properties of something enveloping [...],* something containing? What are things such as τόπος and χώρα, *extension* and *spatium*, based upon?

What is space itself? The answer to this question is simple. But precisely for that reason, what the answer says is difficult to envision and hold onto. For customary opining is only used to considering something to have been clarified once it has been traced back to something

[1] [Written in the manuscript in pencil]: But what then is space itself – its own property? To what extent possible "container?"
* [Word indecipherable.]

else, and once the former thing is explained in terms of the latter one. In contrast, a matter is only experienced in its own property as itself once we forego the process of tracing it back to something else, or once we forego explaining. Instead, the task is to catch sight of the matter in itself and catch sight of what shows itself from out of it.

What is space as space? Answer: space spaces [*Raum räumt*].[2] What does spacing mean? It means clearing out – freeing up, making free. Space can therefore only envelope and contain something because it spaces and because it vacates into the open – and thus it sets limits. Every spatial limit is itself spatial. This [open] grants the possibility of directions in space and the possibility of limits, though it must be kept in mind that the limit itself is spatial.

If we attend to the most unique property of space, namely that it spaces, only then will we be capable of observing a state of affairs which it was never before possible to see in thinking. Spatial: spacing. The way in which the human is in space – it is not like a body. Rather, the human is in space in the way that he grants space [*einräumt*], i.e. permits the open and admits himself and his things – the way in which he orders.

The human is cleared up, radiant, open, and free, or – what in essence amounts to the same thing – the human is opened up. Human Dasein is spatial in a particular characteristic sense. The human is spatial in terms of clearing out the space and thereby admitting the things which he encounters in the open.

The circumscribing of the human is not determined by the outer surface of his body, rather by that among which and at which he resides by clearing out space. [...]*

Clearing space in the double sense, admitting in, and this as well: letting itself be said, what is attributed to him.

Language – saga – concealing and sheltering, all indicators.

Everything is language and not qua articulation, rather out of art: form – content art? – ποίησις.

---

[2] {TN: I have chosen a phrasing that mimics Heidegger's tautological formulation. An alternative rendering of the verb *räumen* would be "to clear space."}

* [Approximately 11 words indecipherable.]

Art and Space[2]

Presumably,[3] the unique attribute of art is attributable to the role it plays in serving as a harbinger, which brings the concealment of being through the work to a destinally bound, but decisive and pathbreaking unconcealment (illuminating). Serving as a harbinger in this way, it shows the human the place of his sojourn within unconcealment, while also playing a role in creating that very place.

In the great epochs of art, when art masters its own power, it requires no aid in the form of statements which deal with art and speak about art.[4]

There was no theory and no literature about art in the age of high Greek art. The poetry of Homer and Pindar, Aeschylus and Sophocles, the buildings and sculptures of the great masters, they all spoke for themselves. They spoke, if "speaking" here means: revealing, showing assignation, and designation. Art enabled the humans of its time to perceive the source from which the human receives his calling. The works of these artists were not the expression of social arrangements, nor testaments to a culture, and they were certainly not descriptions of the experiences of the soul. These works spoke as the indicating echo of the voice, which determined the whole of the existence of this astounding people across a few short centuries. That voice attuned the Greek human into their particular attunement, an attunement which is named with the word αἰδώς. We translate that word in a rough approximation as "awe" in the face of what is unconcealed and, at the same

---

[2] Precursor to the lecture "Art and Space" in *Man and World* 6,1 (1973), 3–8.

[3] Marginal note: questionable limitation: visual art and this in turn only *plastic*; human – life form.

[4] Crossed out: Art itself speaks, if "speaking" here means: making manifest.

time, in the face of what conceals itself in surging forth in presence. Art required no exhibitions. Art itself exposes. It exposes the world in the open revelation of its structure.

In the meantime, after two and a half centuries, Hegel's dictum seems to have come true: "We may well hope that art will always rise higher and come to perfection, but the form of art has ceased to be the supreme need of the spirit." What that means to say is: "For us art counts no longer as the highest mode in which truth fashions an existence for itself."[5]

Up until today no viable justification has been provided to refute Hegel's dictum.

The fate of art and its determination in the contemporary age remain open. It is necessary to contemplate that state of affairs. It is possible for that contemplation to become a form of preparatory thinking, developing in terms of a thinking that prepares a terrain within which the question-worthiness of art is unfolded in a more inceptual manner. In what follows, I will offer a few hints which will attempt to provide some directives guiding us toward the question of the unique element of art. For now, I will take a limited perspective focused on the plastic arts. Moreover, this reflection upon the plastic arts will be further restricted to the question of the plastic arts' relation to space.

In looking back to what has already been said, one might hastily point out that today, for example, the visual arts, and above all the plastic arts, seem destined to once again take on their rightful place. They are now assuming a new relation to the world as the industrial landscape, city planning, and architecture all lay claim to the visual arts. The visual arts now play their role in the planning and design of space. For plastic has a particularly distinct relation to space. It understands itself to be an engagement with space.

Admittedly, however, we are dealing with two fundamentally different epochs of the occidental Dasein of the human – a human who has now become global. The awakening and shaping of the world of the Greek polis in the face of the gods is, of course, fundamentally distinct from modern industrial society's self-constitution in the technical-scientific world of the atomic age. The planning of space and structures of various kinds, even including the most extreme form of space travel, are already regarded as an everyday, self-evident process.

Yet – what is space? What does the artist's engagement with space mean? Who can answer these questions for us? One will insist that

[5] Georg Wilhelm Friedrich Hegel, *Aesthetics: Lectures on Fine Art*, trans. T. M. Knox (Oxford: Clarendon Press, 1975), 103.

the artist himself is best informed about the aforementioned state of affairs. For he *executes* an engagement with space. But can the artist, in and through the execution of this engagement, know with sufficient clarity what occurs in such an engagement? Can the sculptor as sculptor say, i.e. can he say through one of the pieces of his work, what space is and what the engagement with space [calls for]?

The sculptor cannot do that. This incapacity does not indicate a weakness, rather it is the very strength of the artist. The sculptor can say what the visual arts are through his sculpture just as little as the physicist as physicist can say what physics is through his research. For physics cannot be examined in the mode of physics, nor with the tools of physics. Physics as a science is not a potential object for a physics experiment.

What the visual arts are and what art as such is, those are things which cannot be defined by means of a chisel and hammer, or a paint and brush, but they also cannot by defined with the aid of work produced by means of those tools. The visual arts as such are not a possible topic for artistic production. Painting cannot be painted. It is not something colorful.

Here we stumble across a curious state of affairs. Even more curious is the fact that it hardly even unsettles us at all. One might attempt to rescue oneself by escaping into what is apparently self-evident and declare something like this: "Art is what is made by significant artists." But then the follow-up questions would already be in place: Who is an artist? Evidently, the artist is he who satisfies the claim of art. And who is a significant artist? It is not the artist most often traded and sold, rather the artist who satisfies the highest claim to art. But what is art? According to the proposition above, it is what significant artists make.

Thus it becomes clear: the proposition is spinning around in a circle. Neither does it say anything about art, nor about the artist. This proposition does not contemplate what it says and even less so does it contemplate the manner in which it says what it says, namely in a circular movement. The proposition is thoughtless and is nonetheless taken to be illuminating.

The Work of Art and "Art History"

"Works of art" – not the ones that have been, rather the ones that are now "made" – are productions within an environment of creation that was once necessary. This environment has now become a domain of *cultural politics*.

Nowadays, *art works* are first of all "evaluated"; if "evaluations" come first, then that means that the "works" no longer shelter any truth as power within them, rather the works are initially found [*be-funden*] in some arbitrary state and only subsequently acquire *validity* through an equally arbitrary process.

And even if this evaluation amounts to nothing more than the declaration "not bad" – if this alone is already a success and marks an achievement, then even the evaluation has lost its decisive power and is only a makeshift remedy to prevent "art" as "cultural activity" from disappearing entirely, even though the disappearance of the entire enterprise would be the only clean and decisive way to move forward.

Yet on top of all of this, if we still attend to the fact that, in an age which has cultivated the highest ingenuity in appropriating the earliest and most ancient influences and has cultivated such a highly developed capacity for mixing all of these influences together in order to provoke some sort of stimulation from this mixture, an age which is capable of actually achieving something which has never before existed in the mastery of "forms" of process and design – then in such an age the evaluation of "not bad" is only made in reference to this "talent" and the "content" may be completely negligible. Or perhaps – and this would amount to the same thing – the content could even be replaced by mere "topics" motivated by current worldviews, bits of knowledge, and current affairs. At that point the "work" would truly be lacking any necessity.

Only this can explain the fact that the cultural enterprise gains free rein in such ages. And only this can explain why it is that this enterprise is permitted at all to invoke the past, as if its greatness could only be secured by the mercies of contemporary ingenuity.

Reflection upon the Essence and Conduct of the Art-Historical "Science"

What kind of "science" is this? Is it simply historiography [*Historie*] applied to the history [*Geschichte*] of art? What is *art* and what *history* does art have?

Or it is possible to pose the question in this way, framing it in accordance with art and its history: is the historical knowledge of art unique, specifically when this knowledge purports to participate in deciding the *destiny of art*? (To what extent can knowledge "play a role in deciding?") According to which standards should the reflection upon this "science" even take place? Is the reflection still free? (Where does this common principle belong: "Science" must "serve the people?" Can something be said about "science" from this perspective, or has everything about it already been decided so that it can go on to "serve" – but to serve what end? And *what is the people?*)

This is the misrecognition of the historical moment in which the Occidental destiny of art currently stands. This misrecognition involves the rejection of reflection upon art and the rejection of knowledge about art. It also requires elevating the invocation of the "healthy emotion of the people" to a standard for art.

Yet, at the same time, there is a great deal of "theorizing" on the "theory" of art taken to an extreme degree, while the "genius" is assigned a decisive role in this theory.

The *complete bewilderment* of thinking shows itself in all of this (being German – according to Nietzsche: *not wanting any clarity*).[6]

---

[6] Friedrich Nietzsche, *The Birth of Tragedy and The Case of Wagner*, trans. Walter Kaufmann (New York: Vintage, 1967), 177: "… that among the Germans clarity is an objection, logic a refutation."

It is an internal impossibility to seek to decide about the future of art and to know about that future and, at the same time, to continually parade out Wagner as essential art today.

What justifies the rejection of knowledge and inquiry into art? It is solely justified by the shortsighted orientation toward the art business dominant in the last decades. (Glass palace – repetition – rejection of art journalism! As if in German thinking there were no critique of the power of judgment, nor any trace of Hegel's aesthetics, nor Schelling's aesthetics, and as if Nietzsche had never existed.) The orientation toward journalism as *the* sole form of knowledge about art now has the effect of being the sole stance toward knowledge as such. This journalism is rejected – apparently rightly so – and yet this rejection is deeply untrue and ahistorical. But this rejection is also reinforced by a fundamental attitude which simply produces this outcome – it leads to the rejection of all questioning. One does not want to know who we are; or one believes they have decided this question for all eternity.

Very particular opinions are decisive in all of this, and they are predominately a bunch of liberalistic opinions:

1. art is representation – *depiction* of something beautiful viewed beforehand.
2. art is made by the "*genius*" – the "personality" (were there "personalities" among the Greeks and in the Middle Ages?).
3. art serves as *reinforcement* for the authority of the state, and it is manipulated as a means of *asserting* the will of the state and as *propaganda*.
4. the art business is *organized* – as "expression" of the "worldview."
5. the art-temple – *museum*!

In all of this, there is nothing of the originary *historical necessity*, rather everything is based on a sacrosanct dogmatism rooted in political power – nothing at all is based on the power which art itself radiates due to its rootedness in the essential necessities of beyng.

But one could take that all as a transition, and one could say that this transition must necessarily move within the past and within pre-established forms. Certainly – this possibility seems to be given to us and yet it is not – because everything, including one's own *theorizing*, is presented as if it were decisive for all eternity. Consequently, all originary willing is crippled, while only the machination affirms and "gets things done."

Today there could be no transition which would not have the will to take ultimate decisions, i.e. the will to *listen* to *grounded reasons – belonging to listening* as highest freedom.

But now what is supposed to occur? And what could take place at the very place where a form of knowledge of art and of its history is still cultivated – in "art history as a science?"

But a question pre-empts and permeates this entire endeavor: *Which knowledge is supposed to be communicated here?* What kind of reflection is to be awakened, reinforced, and prepared in service of creative force?

The answer is: reflection upon the moment in which the destiny of art is standing. Is art still necessary, i.e. does art arise from a plight? Do we still have the will and the vigor to experience and withstand such a plight? Can we still withstand the plight of the flight of the gods, the plight of the abandonment of being? Only if everything essential attempts to contribute to this reflection, would this outdated enterprise still retain any form of meaning or justification: knowledge of history, the plentitude of works, their *past existence*. Does anything still deserve to be called a "work?" *Is* there still truly a work – and if not, what is a work?

We should not be deceived into thinking that the level of artistic dexterity is increasing as a result of the accumulation of technical capacity in general, nor should we be deceived into thinking that *qualities* are now achievable which exceed earlier levels of mediocrity and that, nonetheless, or indeed *precisely for that very reason*, the great *necessary traits* of the "works" and the works themselves are dwindling according to the same measure – a measure based on the search for "quality" or "topics." The ambiguity, which is the result of a political and state-issued mandate – as if that guaranteed something, whereas – among the Greeks – the πόλις and the ἀγών belonged to the gods and belonged to their truth. And the Greeks did not at all rage about like some form of imperialism or Hellenism of the Roman sort – and in the meantime the entire modern downfall advances on.

How should reflection in the genuine work of science be carried out?

By no means as an *additive project* – as something in the "introduction" or something tacked on to the "conclusion" of "lectures," rather it must occur inconspicuously: in the manner of posing questions [*Fragestellung*], in the manner of historical memory of what is essential and decisive. Undertaking this requires the renunciation of immediate impact. The solitary ones – they alone will have the power to continue carrying the torch of knowledge in darkness.

The courage to master the handiwork all the way from the ground up and to foster it in the future, and yet to completely set it aside – not in the service of the people, but instead in the service of essential knowledge. For essential knowledge "serves" the people by playing a small role in first bringing the people to itself.

And, ultimately, the task is to withstand the way in which all of this willing will simply be chalked up as a "reaction," misconstrued as esoteric, and minimized as nothing but a form of weakness which can nowhere be realized in "actions."

But the essential prevailings of history make no noise and do not require the loud confirmation of the "people."

Editor's Afterword

The present volume contains notes carefully preserved over years from the papers of Martin Heidegger entitled "On the Essence of Language" and published within Division III of the *Complete Works*. Those notes are supplemented by notes on the question of art. The volume begins with sketches on language and then moves to other topics, including an analysis of the craft of language and an analysis of art.

The present volume provides new insights into Heidegger's thinking of language from the late 1930s up until the volume "On the Way to Language." The *Contributions to Philosophy* (GA 65) concluded with emphatic references to both the question of the origin of language and the origin of the work of art, while the volume first published in 1959 (now GA 12) introduced insights developed after 1950 which Heidegger had presented in the form of lectures – with the exception of a passage from a "Conversation on Language" and the 1953 contribution published in *Merkur*.

The texts published here are previously unpublished, with two exceptions. The volume contains treatises and notes on language of varying lengths, a fully developed but hitherto unknown treatise entitled "The Word – On the Essence of Language," as well as an illuminating sketch on art and the academic study of art.

The editor had a number of different sets of documents at his disposal for the production of the manuscripts. These will be described in brief.

The manuscript with the title "The Saga" is contained in a slipcase with the label "16: George. Contemporary Poets III Cloth-Binding" and is identified with the signature B 29 a. The pages are numbered at the bottom left in pencil, ranging from 1–89, and are also numbered at the top right, ranging from 1–44. A note refers to a copy of the manuscript in "Green Folder 7." The individual sections are also furnished with headings. The editor adopted these headings. The date "1942" in the list presumably indicates the year of origin. Fritz Heidegger produced the transcription. The envelope containing the manuscript is marked with the reference: "Prose Lectures – From the History of Beyng. On Hölderlin. Including: 'The Saga'. 44 pages stapled."

The treatise entitled "The Word. On the Essence of Language" and an envelope containing it are held in an orange-colored folder marked with the signature C 21. The folder is entitled "On the Essence of Language (Sketch of an Intimation)." The title of the main text contained there is: "The Birth of Language." Next to the final draft, which contains only sparse corrections, there is a copy of a manuscript numbered by hand (a second final draft) on the same topic, also contained in the envelope of that name. According to a note, the text was presented as a gift to "Frau Margot von Meiningen, On Her Birthday 1945."

The full title for the sketches contained together in the blue folder also labelled C 21 is: "The Word – The Sign – The Conversation – Language." On the envelope there is a reference to a two-hour advanced graduate seminar from the summer semester 1939 entitled "The Word and Language." It also contains a supplement in a different handwriting: "Seminar on Herder's 'Origin of Language' – fully elaborated MS (in IV)" (see Ingrid Schüßler's "Afterword" to GA 85, p. 217). At the top right the word "E[reignis]" is written. The individual pages are numbered with pencil at the bottom left. – The copies of the sections are labelled with Roman numerals, the sections themselves are labelled sequentially with Arabic numerals.

The ten sections of this collection of papers bear the following titles: I. *The Word and Language*, II. *The Sign (its Essence Bound to the Event)*, III. *The Word: The Conversation and Language*, IV. *The Word (cf. Poetry and Thinking)*, V. *The Word and Language*, VI. *Word and "Language,"* VII. *The Essential Prevailing of the Word*, VIII. *Image and Sound – The Sensible*, IX. *Language*, X. *Language*.

The text which has already been published under the title "The Word: The Meaning of Words" (129–132, with the "Preliminary Remark," 133 and Title Page, 134) is inserted into section IV. The first edition of the text is published in Dietrich Papenfuss and Otto Pöggeler, eds., *Im Spiegel der Welt: Sprache, Übersetzung, Auseinandersetzung (Zur philosophischen Aktualität Heideggers)*, vol. 3 (Frankfurt am Main: Vittorio Klostermann, 1992), pp. 13–16. The manuscript used as the source for the publication is contained in the folder in duplicate, once with transcription addenda in the margins and once without the addenda. The brief collection of paper "Language" was integrated into that manuscript later on. The collection bears the heading: "'Remark' – On Haman's Dictum: 'Reason is Language, logos'."

The text on the two poems by Eduard Mörike was previously published in the annual publication of the Martin-Heidegger-Gesellschaft in 2004. The editorial afterward to that edition states:

> At the invitation of the Pedagogical Academy II of Freiburg, Martin Heidegger led an evening conversation on July 12, 1955 about Mörike's poems "September Morning" and "At Midnight." In 1973 Heidegger had the manuscript of the sketch made into a typewritten copy by his assistant at the time, the editor of Martin-Heidegger-Gesellschaft's annual publication. The manuscript for this edition was prepared based on the photocopied manuscript and the original version. The manuscripts of the sketches are produced here in reprint almost entirely without alteration and with the original numbering. The quotes were checked and adjusted to the editions indicated here. Atypical abbreviations were spelled out. All underling is indicated with italics. (Friedrich-Wilhelm von Herrmann)

The reproduction of the original page numbers had to be abandoned here; a reference to Heidegger's desk copy of Pindar's Odes was added.

The sketches on the topic "Image and Word" are located in the slipcase B 58 ("The 24 Propositions by Leibniz/Tyche/On the Poems by J. P. Hebel, etc." – Divisions III and IV) and in a collection of papers entitled "On 'Alienation' as Delusion." These comprise four blue pages numbered in the top right with pencil, including red highlights/corrections, alongside a page with notes on the "Guiding Threads." The words "First image …" written on a separate sheet help to indicate which section from *Aus der Erfahrung des Denkens* Heidegger is referring to: "First image preserves face. / Yet image rests in the poem" (GA 13, p. 79). These are presumably notes for the introductory presentation for the seminar on the topic "Image and Word," held in early summer 1960 in Bremen in the Bremer Kunsthalle (in front of works by Rembrandt and Manessier), as well as in the Haus am Lindenweg (Obernauland). Heinrich W. Petzet chronicles the latter event in Heinrich W. Petzet, *Encounters and Dialogues with Martin Heidegger, 1929–1976* (Chicago: University of Chicago Press, 1993), pp. 59ff.

The sketch "On the Question of Art" is located in slipcase B 58 ("The 24 Propositions of Leibniz …" see above) in the collection of papers entitled "Space and Place." Pagination is located at the top left

(6 pages). An additional page, not reproduced here, is marked with notes and the reference "St. G." in the top left and on the six pages separated by a slash, seems to belong here ("Sankt Gallen," according to Hermann Heidegger).

The text "Art and Space" contains five pages held in the folder "chamois 14." The pages are written along the left-hand side with corrections, with remarks and additions contained on the right. According to handwritten notes, this is a preliminary stage to the lecture "Art and Space" (printed in GA 14, p. 203–210; English: *Man and World* 6,1 (1973), pp. 3–8).

"Work of Art and Art History" belongs to the collection B 84: "On the Origin of the Work of Art" (blue paperboard). It contains drafts of lectures from the years 1935 and 1936. This text is inserted into the separate collection of papers with the title "The Origin of the Work of Art. Frankfurt Lectures Sep./Dec. 1936." This note is located at the bottom: "III. Draft – cf. lecture on Nietzsche from the Winter Semester, above all fundamentals on 'Aesthetics' and the Knowledge of Art, pp. 30ff." (cf. GA 43). The two pages are numbered at the top right with a fountain pen. Inserted behind them is a copy of the following essay: "Reflection upon the Essence and Conduct of the Art-Historical 'Science.' The location information is also collection B 84: "On the Origin of the Work of Art" (blue paperboard). These comprise nine pages numbered at the top right (with the abbreviations for Art [*Kunst – K., Ku.*] and Art History [*Kunstgeschichte – Kg.*]).

In the reproduction of the text, the peculiarities of Heidegger's writing style have been maintained throughout. Abbreviations have been spelled out, especially when they refer to Heidegger's own texts and manuscripts. The use of symbols has been augmented here and there, underlining is set in italics, and the structure of paragraphs is consistently organized in accordance with the originals. References to other manuscripts and texts by Heidegger are supplemented by references to the volumes of the *Complete Works*.

Description of the Individual Texts

The sketches gathered under the title "The Saga" revolve around questions which relate to the "Reference of Language to Beyng" (*Contributions to Philosophy*, pp. 392–393). Several notes develop into shorter treatises and attempt, from the standpoint of the intuited "first inception," to reveal how the metaphysics of language and linguistics are bound to a set of presuppositions.

The "Sketch of an Intimation" from the *Essence of Language* is a very intensive, self-contained treatise which, in a very dense manner, takes the proximity of poetry and thinking literally, approaching them from the perspective of thinking and probing their common dialogue with one another. The addenda supplement this text, which is published here for the first time, with references to closely related phenomena such as silence and stillness, but especially to Hölderlin, the poet who had a decisive influence on Heidegger's thinking about language.

The drafts preserved in the long collection of papers with the title "The Word – The Conversation – The Sign – Language" return repeatedly, from ever new starting points, to an examination of the characteristics of the word and human understanding itself, dealing with the sound, the character of signs, and their linguistic objectification. This objectification is contrasted with the "event-bound" element of the word in rather melodious formulations. Finally, it attempts to render the mesmerizing spell of the instrumental and "anthropological" conception of language known as such. The "conversation" is designated here as the "homeland of language." Individual references to the literature Heidegger utilized show that he oriented himself on the contemporary debates, including the disputes initiated by Hugo von Hofmannsthal, among others. Numerous references reveal the connection to other sketches from the time, including manuscripts that have hitherto been only partially accessible ("Variations," "Ponderings"), but they also reveal their distance from *Being and Time*. The interweaving of language and freedom was already alluded to in the courses on Herder from the Summer Semester 1939 (GA 85, p. 75f.). In several of the sketches presented here, the "truth of the word" is brought even more decisively into direct connection with the "opening up of freedom" (see especially the third collection of papers, No. 147).

The conversation on Mörike shows how important it was for Heidegger the "educator" to listen to poetry and to read poems intensively "in conversation," without getting bogged down in grammar and logic, or in the "thinking and translation machines" of the art business. On the topic of the "Image and Word," Heidegger does not seek definitions, but instead aims at the clarification of a domain of questioning. Repeated attempts to inquire into this domain are necessary and they require direct engagement with the works whose "speaking" is under analysis in the text.

The sketches on the topic "Art and Space" invoke the unique element of art in its "great age" and move from there to an analysis of the essential element of space, namely that it "clears space," and is precisely not a terrain for the movement of points of mass and I-points. Heidegger claims that propositions about what art is generally do not go beyond a "circular movement." The final text takes aim, with astonishing clarity, at the "art business of the last decades." The text demands a "reflection" upon the "genuine work of science." In order to prevent science from losing its essential form entirely, it can be made to serve the people or other institutions of society just as little as art can.

The goal of the sketches is to find the way back to the peculiar essential ground of language within the context of beyng-historical thinking. Heidegger attempts to step beyond the "sphere of metaphysical reflection" (*Contributions*, p. 392) by embarking on his questions from different points of approach. These texts are especially important not only for understanding Heidegger's thinking in the 1940s, but also for understanding the evermore intrusive impoverishment of language in the scientific-technical world.

A hearty thanks to the administrator of the Heidegger estate, Dr. Hermann Heidegger, for entrusting me with preparing this volume, even under difficult circumstances. My hearty thanks especially to Dr. Hartmut Tietjen, with whom I had the opportunity on multiple occasions to discuss all of the texts in the process of collating in Freiburg and Glottertal. Without his profound knowledge and intimate familiarity with Heidegger's handwriting, many things would have remained unclear. An equally hearty thanks to Professor Friedrich-Wilhelm von Herrmann, whose extensive experience provided inestimable help in the production and organization of the volume. I owe an obliging debt of gratitude to Dr. Ulrich von Bülow (German Literature Archive Marbach) for his amicable support during my stay in Marbach am Neckar. Furthermore, I am deeply indebted to Dr. Konrad Heumann (Freies Deutsches Hochstift) for helpful references, and to Dr. Cathrin Nielsen, who provided many important suggestions while reviewing the proofs. Of course this goes as well for Professor von Herrmann, Dr. Hermann Heidegger, and his wife, Jutta Heidegger, who supported me in an amicable and creative manner during the corrections, drawing on her reservoir of extensive experience with difficult manuscript passages. I thank my son Jakob for his support in copying the typewritten manuscripts.

Offenbach, June 2010   Thomas Regehly

Glossaries

English–German

abysmally grounded; grounded in the abyss	ab-gründig
abyss	Abgrund
abyssal ground	Ab-grund
acoustic sound	Schall
active silence	erschweigen
agreement, communication	Verständigung
answer	Antwort
answering word	Ant-wort
appoint	verabreden
appointment	Verabredung
appropriate, happening of the event	ereignen
articulation, utterance	Äußerung
attune	stimmen
attunement	Stimmung
bear significant meaning, to signify meaning	be-deuten
bearing out, carrying out	Austrag
bearing out, offering	Aus-trag
beingness	Seiendheit
bespeak	ersagen
beyng	Seyn
beyng-historical	seynsgeschichtlich
bound to the event	ereignishaft
cipher	Chiffre
clearing	Lichtung
coincide	übereinstimmen
coincidence	Übereinstimmung

concordance, agreement	Übereinkunft
conversation	Gespräch
correspond	entsprechen
corrupted essence	Unwesen
cradle	Wiege
declaration	Kundgabe
departure	Abschied
departure (in the mode of; in terms of the)	abschiedlich
depict, sketch	zeichnen
directive	Anweisung
discourse, talk	Rede
disquiet	Unruhe
dwell	wohnen
encouragement	Zuspruch
essential occurrence	Wesung
event (of appropriation)	Ereignis
footpath	Steg
grace	Huld
happening of the event	Er-eignis
heal	heilen
historiography	Historie
history	Geschichte
human (being)	Mensch
image	Sinnbild
inception	Anfang
inceptual	anfänglich
indicate	anzeigen
indicate	weisen
indication	Weisung
indicator	Zeignis
initial sounding	Anklang
intimacy	Innigkeit
intimate, hint	winken
intimation, clue	Wink
intone	anstimmen
juncture	Fügung
keep silent	schweigen
mantra, saying	Spruch
mean	bedeuten
meaning	Bedeutung
pliable, compliant	gefügig

plight	Not
point	deuten
point out	andeuten
pointing out	an-deuten
preserve	wahren
preserving truth	Wahr-heit
proclamation	Ansage
promise	versprechen
pronounce	aussprechen
pronouncement	Aussprache
proposition, statement	Aussage
quicken	heitern
quickening (element)	Heiternde
quiet, calm	Ruhe
radiance	(das) Heitere
radiant	heiter
refer	verweisen
reference	Verweisung
refusal	Verweigerung
remembrance	Andenken
resonate	tönen
resplendence	(die) Heitere
reverberation	Widerhall
rift	Riß
risk	wagen
saga	Sage
say	sagen
sense	Sinn
sign	Zeichen
signal	Signal
signification	Bezeichnung
signify	bezeichnen
sound	Laut
sound (out)	klingen
sounding out	lauten
speak	sprechen
steadfastness	Inständigkeit
still, nurse	stillen
stillness	Stille
structure	Gefüge
symbol	Symbol
thought of thanks	Gedank

timbre	Ton
tolling sound	Geläut
tone	Klang
truth	Wahrheit
verbal articulation	Verlautbarung
voice	Stimme
weigh	wägen
weigh, have weight	wiegen
while	Weile
word	Wort

German–English

Abgrund	abyss
Ab-grund	abyssal ground
ab-gründig	abysmally grounded; grounded in the abyss
Abschied	departure
Ab-schiedlich	in the mode of departure
Andenken	remembrance
andeuten	point out; allude
an-deuten	pointing out
Anfang	inception
anfänglich	inceptual
Anklang	initial sounding
Ansage	proclamation
anstimmen	intone
Antwort	answer
Ant-wort	answering word
Anweisung	directive
anzeigen	indicate
Aussage	proposition, statement
Aussprache	pronouncement
aussprechen	pronounce
Äußerung	articulation, utterance
Austrag	bearing out; carrying out
Aus-trag	offering; bearing out
bedeuten	mean
be-deuten	bear significant meaning; to signify meaning
Bedeutung	meaning
bezeichnen	signify

Bezeichnung	signification
Chiffre	cipher
deuten	point
entsprechen	correspond
ereignen	appropriate, happening of the event
Ereignis	event, event of appropriation
Er-eignis	happening of the event
ereignishaft	bound to the event
ersagen	bespeak
erschweigen	active silence
Fügung	juncture
Gedank	thought of thanks
Gefüge	structure
gefügig	pliable, compliant
Geläut	tolling sound
Geschichte	history
Gespräch	conversation
heilen	heal
heiter	radiant
Heitere (das)	radiance
Heitere (die)	resplendence
heitern	quicken
Heiternde	the quickening (element)
Historie	historiography
Huld	grace
Innigkeit	intimacy
Inständigkeit	steadfastness
Klang	tone
klingen	sound (out)
Kundgabe	declaration
Laut	sound
lauten	sounding out
Lichtung	clearing
Mensch	human, human being
Not	plight
Rede	discourse, talk
Riß	rift
Ruhe	quiet, calm
Sage	saga
sagen	say
Schall	acoustic sound

schweigen	keep silent
Seiendheit	beingness
Seyn	Beyng
Seynsgeschichtlich	beyng-historical
Signal	signal
Sinn	sense
Sinnbild	image
sprechen	speak
Spruch	mantra, saying
Steg	footpath
Stille	stillness
stillen	still, nurse
Stimme	voice
stimmen	attune
Stimmung	attunement
Symbol	symbol
Ton	timbre
tönen	resonate
Übereinkunft	concordance, agreement
übereinstimmen	coincide
Übereinstimmung	coincidence
Unruhe	disquiet
Unwesen	corrupted essence
verabreden	appoint
Verabredung	appointment
Verlautbarung	verbal articulation
versprechen	promise
Verständigung	agreement, communication
Verweigerung	refusal
verweisen	refer
Verweisung	reference
wagen	to risk
wägen	to weigh
wahren	preserve
Wahrheit	truth
Wahr-heit	preserving truth
Weile	while
weisen	indicate
Weisung	indication
Wesung	essential occurrence
Widerhall	reverberation
Wiege	cradle

wiegen	to weigh; to have weight
Wink	intimation, clue
winken	intimate, hint
wohnen	to dwell
Wort	word
Wort – plural: Worte	words
Wort – plural: Wörter	vocabulary words; vocabulary
Zeichen	sign
zeichnen	depict, sketch
Zeignis	indicator
Zuspruch	encouragement